RUNNING PRESS
# GEM

---

# FLAGS

---

A Guide to More Than 200
*Flags of the World*

Carol P. Shaw

Running Press
Philadelphia, Pennsylvania

First published in the United States of America in 1994 by
Running Press Book Publishers.

Originally published by HarperCollins Publishers Limited under the
title *Collins Gem Flags*

9 8 7 6 5 4 3 2 1
Digit on the right indicates the number of this printing.

ISBN: 1-56138-384-8

Library of Congress Cataloging-in-Publication Number: 93-085523

Cover design by Toby Schmidt

Printed in Italy by Amadeus S.p.A.

This book may be ordered by mail from your publisher. Please
include $2.50 for postage and handling. *But try your bookstore first!*

Running Press Book Publishers
125 South Twenty-second Street
Philadelphia, Pennsylvania 19103-4399

# Introduction

## The history of flags

Flags and flag-like emblems have been used for over 5,000 years with their styles, shapes and appearances constantly changing throughout that time. Flags were first used during war and at sea, for purposes of identification. The earliest-recorded flag-like objects, called vexilloids, were solid objects, often models of animals and birds or abstract shapes, held aloft on poles. These were used not only as rallying banners but were attributed with the power to grant protection and victory to their bearers. Vexilloids were used by the Romans (for example, in the eagle standards of the legions), but the Romans were also the first to introduce cloth banners to the West.

Flags were used by the Crusaders fighting Islamic forces in the Holy Land in the 12th and 13th centuries, and it was in these circumstances of a "holy war" that many of the flags which are familiar today had their origins. The Cross was an obvious symbol which united the Europeans, and heraldic rules were devised to regulate the proliferation of similar designs (see overleaf). Rectangular banners, hung from vertical rather than horizontal poles, were more practical than earlier long, trailing pennants, and began to be used more regularly.

The banners used in Europe throughout the Middle Ages generally represented monarchs, families or cities, but not countries, as nations were expected to identify with the flags of their monarchs. National flags as distinct entities did not emerge clearly until the 17th century with, for example, the creation in 1606 of the first flag of Great Britain after the 1603 union of Scotland and England under James VI and I. Most of the flags in use today evolved from the nationalist and revolutionary movements of the 18th and 19th centuries.

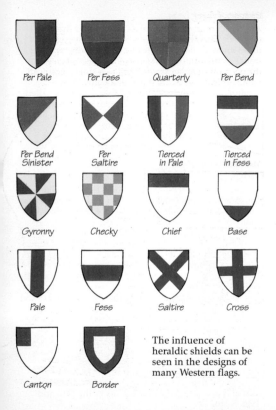

Per Pale

Per Fess

Quarterly

Per Bend

Per Bend Sinister

Per Saltire

Tierced in Pale

Tierced in Fess

Gyronny

Checky

Chief

Base

Pale

Fess

Saltire

Cross

Canton

Border

The influence of heraldic shields can be seen in the designs of many Western flags.

### Shapes of flags

Almost all modern flags are rectangular in shape, but this is a relatively recent convention. In medieval times many different shapes were common, ranging from a pennant tied to the top of a knight's lance, to the pennants and streamers fixed to a ship's masthead. Some typical shapes are illustrated below, and

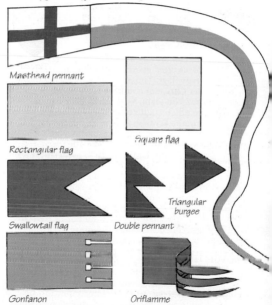

Masthead pennant

Rectangular flag

Square flag

Swallowtail flag

Double pennant

Triangular burgee

Gonfanon

Oriflamme

examples of all these can still be seen today. Switzerland's flag, for example, is square, while the the Nepalese flag is of a double pennant design. Triangular burgees are usually flown on yachts, while swallowtail flags, usually with a tongue (i.e. a third pointed tail, between the other two) are used particularly in Scandinavian countries, as naval ensigns. More unusual designs, such as gonfanons and oriflammes, being medieval flags, can still be seen nowadays in pageants and displays.

## The symbolism of flags

Common themes and meanings can be seen in flags, and these ideas often exert an influence on the designs of new flags. The most obvious theme in the flags of older Christian countries is the motif of the Cross: this may be plain, as in the English flag, a saltire (generally recognized as the symbol of a martyr), as in the Scottish flag, or an off-centered cross, such as those used in the Scandinavian countries. Another popular design is the tricolor: first adopted in the Netherlands, it was its association with the French revolutionaries of 1789 which charged it with a significance for subsequent movements seeking revolutionary change and independence. Tricolors, arranged horizontally or vertically, remain the most popular flag design today.

The use of color, too, is often symbolic in flags. Red is a color associated with both Communism and Socialism, but it can also mean danger or revolution. White means both peace and surrender; orange is generally taken to represent courage and sacrifice; green signals safety and permission to proceed, as well as being associated with the Islamic religion; yellow signifies sickness and the need for caution; and black represents mourning, death and anarchy.

Groups of colors are also used by nations to express a particular purpose or aspiration. The blue, white and red of the French and American flags were associated with revolution and freedom, and were often adopted by countries seeking independence from imperial rule in the 19th century. Red, yellow and green, originally the colors of Ethiopia, were used by Ghana and then by other newly independent African nations in the 1950s and '60s, and came to express freedom and a desire for African unity; these were known as the Pan-African colors. Similar sentiments were expressed in the Pan-Arab colors of red, white, black and green, used in the flags of many of the states around the Persian Gulf as they emerged into independence after centuries of Turkish Ottoman domination. The white, blue and red of Russia, too, came to be used by the Pan-Slav movement in eastern Europe in the mid 19th century to represent a desire for freedom from the Hapsburg Empire. Some of these Slav flags reappeared after the dissolution of the Union of Soviet Socialist Republics (USSR) and Yugoslavia, and the partition of Czechoslovakia.

The Russian white, blue and red was superseded by the new flag of the USSR after the Russian Revolution of 1917. This was a version of the traditional red flag of

Socialism and revolution, with the addition of a yellow star of internationalism and a crossed hammer and sickle, representing industry and agriculture (see p. 7). The color and the design were adapted for use by Communist and Socialist countries across the world, with local equivalents of the hammer and sickle being used wherever the flag was adopted. Although the USSR ceased to exist at the end of 1991 and its flag is no longer used officially, it remains one of the most striking and influential flags of the 20th century.

## Purposes of flags

Although identification and decoration were among the primary purposes of early flags, they came to acquire a symbolism of their own when displayed for a particular cause or event. Consequently, they are used now in official expressions of celebration, of mourning (flown at half mast or draped over coffins) or for decorative purposes. However, the main function of flags is still that of symbols for identification and expressions of unity.

Of course, it is not only nation states which have their own flags. All kinds of organizations, from military and civic to religious, political, and industrial, have their own banners – in fact, a flag can be used by any group of people to express a common interest or purpose. Most towns, cities and provinces have their own flags, while all heads of state – monarchs and presidents – have their emblems, too. Among the best-known non-national flags are those of international organizations such as the United Nations, with its symbolic olive wreath surrounding the world, the Olympic flag, with the five interlinked circles representing the five continents, and the flags of the Geneva Convention, the Red Cross and the Red Crescent.

Flag of the International Federation of Vexillological Associations

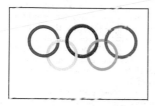

Olympic Flag

Flag of the United Nations

Flags have also been used for signalling. Semaphore is a system generally used on land, although a type of semaphore is also used at sea over short distances. Signal codes, with flags representing numbers, were developed for use at sea during the 18th century, and the International Code has continually been improved and modified since its introduction in 1857. It initially included 70,000 signals and used 18 flags. Each flag signifies a letter of the alphabet and, when flown singly, has a separate meaning of its own. Sailors still have to learn how to hoist and read signals correctly, even though modern methods of communication might seem to have rendered them obsolete.

Below are shown substitutes which allow the same signal flag, either alphabetical or numerical, to be repeated one or more times in the same group.

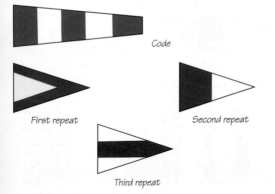

Code

First repeat

Second repeat

Third repeat

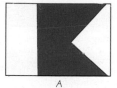

A

B

C

D

E

F

G

H

I

J

K

L

M

N

O

P

Q

K

S

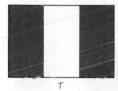

T

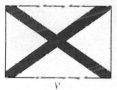

U

V

W

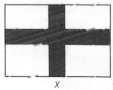

X

Y

Z

1

2

3

4

5

6

7

8

9

0

## Parts of a flag

When flags are shown, the flagpole is normally assumed to be on the left of the observer's view. The side then visible is called the *obverse*, the other being the *reverse*. For design and orientation purposes, flags are said to be divided into four quarters, each of which is called a *canton*. The two cantons by the pole are known as the *hoist*, and the other two are called the *fly*. Perhaps confusingly, the upper hoist canton (where many design features on flags are located) is simply referred to as the *canton*. The standard measurements of a flag, given as a proportion of width to length, constitute its *ratio;* ratios are given for flags throughout the book.

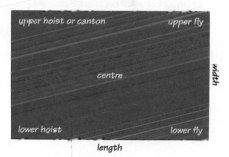

## Glossary

**Arms**: The official heraldic symbols of a nation or family, including a shield with distinctive devices and often supporters (figures on either side of the shield), a crest (a heraldic symbol above the shield) and other insignia. Normally, arms appear on a flag in a simplified form, e.g. with just the shield.

**Banner**: A flag bearing a coat of arms or one hanging from a crossbar or between two poles. Figuratively, it can refer to any type of flag.

**Battle honor**: An inscription on military colors designed to show the particular successes of a unit in combat.

**Bicolor**: A flag of two bands of color, arranged horizon-tally or vertically; e.g. see Monaco.

**Bunting**: A type of plain weave material used in the manufacture of flags. Also a string of decorative small flags.

**Burgee**: A triangular or swallowtail flag used by ships and boats, particularly yachts to indicate membership of a particular yacht club.

**Canton**: An area of a flag or shield obtained by dividing its field with a horizontal and vertical line; used particularly to refer to the quarter in the upper left corner.

**Charge**: A figure or symbol appearing in the field of a flag or a shield.

**Civil flag**: The national flag used by private citizens on land. Civil flags have been used rather than state flags throughout this book to illustrate national flags.

**Coat of arms**: See **Arms**.

**Colors**: The flag of a military unit, such as a regiment. Metaphorically speaking, it also refers to the flag of a country.

**Counterchange**: To reverse two colors on either side of a line on a flag as, for example, in the crosses of St. Andrew and St. Patrick on the Union Jack.

**Dexter**: On the right-hand side of a shield or flag when seen from a bearer's viewpoint, so on the left-hand side as seen by a viewer.

**Emblem**: A device often used as a charge on a flag, but which can also be used separately. It is used to represent a nation, city, family or an idea. It may be of heraldic origin or may be more modern, e.g. the maple leaf on the Canadian flag.

**Ensign**: A national flag flown at or near the stern of a ship. A country may have a civil ensign (for use on civil and merchant ships), state ensign (for use on non-military vessels) and naval ensign (flown on warships).

**Field**: The background of a flag or a shield.

**Fimbriation**: A narrow edging or border, often in white, on a flag to separate two other colors.

**Flag**: A piece of cloth, usually attached to a pole or staff, decorated with a design and used for purposes of identification, symbolizing, signalling, etc.

**Flag of convenience**: A flag of a particular country flown by a foreign ship registered there to take advantage of that nation's weaker financial or legal regulations.

**Fly**: The outer edge of a flag; usually referring to the half furthest away from the flagpole.

**Half-mast**: The hanging of a flag below the top of a flagpole to indicate mourning or distress. This leaves room for death's flag above.

**Hoist**: The edge of a flag nearest the flagpole; usually referring to the half nearest the pole. Also meaning raise a flag.

**International Code**: A means of signalling by the use of flags representing specific letters of the alphabet.

**Jack**: A small flag flown at the bow of a ship to indicate nationality.

**Jolly Roger**: A flag traditionally used by pirates and comprising a white skull above two crossed bones set on a black field.

**Length**: The measurement of a flag along the side at right angles to the flagpole.

**Obverse**: The more important side of a flag, visible when the flagpole is on the viewer's left.

**National flag**: See **Civil flag**, **State flag**.

**Pennant**: A small tapering or triangular flag, used especially on ships for identification or signalling; also used as a souvenir or decoration.

**Rank flag**: A flag, generally used in the armed forces, to indicate the status of an officer.

**Ratio**: A flag's proportions described as relative width to length.

**Reverse**: The less important side of a flag, seen when the flagpole is on the observer's right.

**Semaphore**: A means of signalling by holding a flag in each hand and moving the arms to designated positions denoting letters of the alphabet.

**Sinister**: On the left-hand side of a shield or flag when seen from a bearer's viewpoint, or the right-hand side as seen by a viewer.

**Standard**: A flag of any kind, including a vexilloid, medieval banner, heraldic or military flag, or the banner of a noble or a head of state.

**State flag**: The national flag flown on land by official and government organizations. Where these differ from civil flags, they normally carry the national arms. The flags illustrated throughout this book are civil flags.

**Swallowtail**: A flag on which a triangular portion has been cut from the fly. One with a double triangular cut is called a swallowtail with tongue. This style of flag is used particularly in the ensigns of the Scandinavian countries.

**Triband**: A flag of two colors used in three bands which are arranged horizontally or vertically; e.g. see Austria.

**Tricolor**: A flag of three bands of different color which are arranged horizontally or vertically; e.g. see France.

**Vexilloid**: An emblem, either solid (such as the standard of a Roman legion) or cloth (such as a flag).

**Vexillology**: The study of flags and their history.

**Width**: The measurement of a flag down the side parallel to the flagpole.

# AFGHANISTAN, Islamic State of

FLAG RATIO 1:2

The victory in April 1992 in the civil war by the mujaheddin, the fundamentalist Muslim guerillas, resulted in a new set of national colors for Afghanistan. The traditional black, red and green tri-color, used since 1929, was replaced by a new green, white and black pattern. These were the colors used by the mujaheddin in the war. The new national arms, added to the flag in December 1992, retain some of the elements used in the past, such as the Muslim *mihrab* (a niche in a mosque wall, indicating the direction of Mecca) and a *minabar* (a pulpit). These are surrounded by wheat wreaths (representing agriculture) bound by a ribbon. To these have been added slogans of the Islamic militants: Allah-o-Akbar (God is Great), which appears just above the mosque, and the *shahada*, or Islamic creed, written between the tips of the wreaths of wheat. These slogans also appear on the flags of Iran, Iraq and Saudi Arabia. The date above the scroll is 1371 (1992 AD), the date in the Muslim calendar when the mujaheddin achieved victory.

# ALBANIA, *Republic of*

FLAG RATIO 5:7

The symbol of the two-headed black eagle which
appears on a red field on the Albanian flag echoes the
flag of Skanderbeg, the 15th-century leader against
Turkish occupation of the country. The word
"Albania" itself means "land of the eagle." This
emblem also had been used to represent the
Byzantine Empire of the 5th–15th centuries, of which
Albania was a part. A yellow-fimbriated red star, symbol of Communism, was added in 1946 after the successful Communist-led fight for freedom from Italian
occupation during the Second World War, but this
was dropped in 1992 after the fall of Communism.

# ALGERIA, Democratic and Popular Republic of

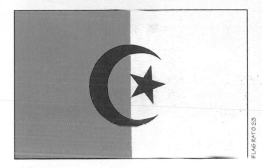

The national flag of Algeria was officially adopted when the country won its independence from France in 1962. Conflicting stories exist to explain its origins: traditionally it was said to have been used by patriots fighting against French colonization in the first half of the 19th century. However, it is now thought more likely that it was designed for the National Liberation Movement (Front de Libération National) in 1928, being used in the struggle for independence from then on. The green of the hoist is the traditional color of Islam; the white in the fly represents purity; and the red crescent and star over them are recognized as a symbol of Islam, their color symbolizing the blood of national heroes.

# AMERICAN SAMOA

FLAG RATIO 1:2

The eastern part of the archipelago of Samoa was a dependency of the United States of America from 1899, and achieved self-government as an overseas territory in 1960. The flag was adopted in the same year. The American bald eagle clutching a chief's staff and a knife, traditional Samoan symbols of authority, signifies American protection of Samoa. The colors against which this motif appears – blue, red and white – are the colors of the American flag.

# ANDORRA, Co-principality of

FLAG RATIO 2:3

Said to have been based on the French tricolor, the national flag of Andorra was adopted in 1866. The principality has been under Franco–Spanish suzerainty since 1278, and the colors of its flag reflect those of its protectors. The Andorran coat of arms appears in the center of the yellow strip, and consists of a quartered shield depicting the miter and crozier of the Spanish Bishops of Urgel, the arms (three stripes of red on yellow) of the French counts of Foix (the bishops and the counts being Andorra's traditional protectors and joint princes), four red stripes on yellow from the arms of Catalonia, and two cows from the arms of Béarn. A motto, Virtus Unita Fortior (United Strength is Greater), appears at the base. A new constitution was adopted in 1993 when Andorra joined the United Nations.

# ANGOLA, Republic of

FLAG RATIO 1:2

The national flag, adopted in 1975, was based on the
flag of the Movimiento Popular de Libertação de
Angola (MPLA), the main nationalist group who won
the country's independence after centuries as a
Portuguese colony. The MPLA subsequently formed
the government of Angola. The elements taken from
the MPLA flag are its colors – red, signifying the
struggle for liberty and the blood shed in the fight for
freedom, and black for Africa – and its star, which
represents both Communism and internationalism.
The addition of the half gear wheel and machete,
local variations on the hammer and sickle of the old
Soviet flag, symbolize the importance of industry and
agriculture. The yellow color of the central motif represents the country's wealth.

# ANGUILLA

Anguilla has had an unofficial flag since 1967, when it broke away from the St Christopher-Nevis group which was planning to become fully independent from Britain. In it, a circlet of three orange dolphins, standing for strength, unity and endurance, were set on a white band, representing a desire for peace. A narrower blue band appeared in the lower part of the flag, and symbolized youthfulness and hope. Anguilla became a British colony in its own right, and the design of the unofficial flag was adopted in 1990 for the island's official coat of arms. The arms now appear in the fly of the British Blue Ensign to form the official colonial flag. The old, unofficial flag, however, is still widely used.

# ANTIGUA AND BARBUDA

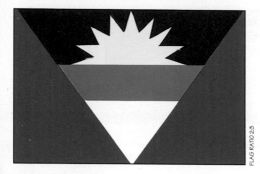

FLAG RATIO 2:3

A competition held in 1967, when the islands became an associated state prior to full independence from Britain, decided the look of the national flag of Antigua and Barbuda. The winning entry comprised two outer triangles of red, a color expressive of the vigor and dynamism of the people, with the golden sun of a new era rising over three stripes of black (signifying both the soil and the people's African heritage), blue (representing hope) and white. The arrangement of these bands with the red triangles forms a "V" shape, the symbol of victory. This design also serves the purpose of promoting the islands' natural attractions – sun, sea and sand (gold, blue and white). The flag continued in use after the islands attained independence in 1981.

# ARGENTINA, Argentine Republic

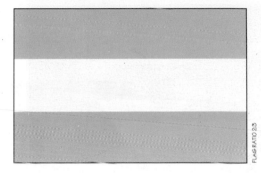

FLAG RATIO 2:3

The colors of the Argentinian flag were identified
with the struggle for liberation from Spain in the 19th
century, and they subsequently influenced the design
of other flags of South and Central American nations.
The Liberation Army of General Manuel Belgrano
wore blue-and-white cockades initially to distinguish
them from Spanish troops, as both had red insignias.
On May 25, 1810, when crowds in Buenos Aires
demanded self-determination from the Spanish
viceroy, the demonstrators, too, wore the cockades,
and the colors were later adopted for the national
flag. The yellow Sun of May, which appears in the
center of the state flag, was taken from the sun
depicted on the first gold coins minted by the new
government in 1810. It was also said to represent both
the sun as it appeared in the skies on May 25 and the
bright future for the newly liberated nation.

# ARMENIA, *Republic of*

FLAG RATIO 1:2

The flag of the Republic of Armenia was adopted in 1990, over a year before the official break-up of the Union of Soviet Socialist Republics, of which the country had recently been a part. Armenia had been an independent nation in modern times from 1918 to 1921, after the break-up of the old empires and before the country's occupation by Bolshevik forces. The flag's colors are symbolic: red represents the blood shed by Armenians particularly in their struggles for existence against the Turks; blue represents the unchanged character of the land; and orange expresses courage through the work of the people. It has been claimed that the colors were also used in ancient flags and banners in the region, as long ago as the 2nd century BC. Like many of the other former Soviet republics, Armenia has retained the ratio of the USSR's old Hammer and Sickle in its new flag, rather than the 2:3 ratio of its own original flag.

# AUSTRALIA, Commonwealth of

FLAG RATIC '12

As with many of the former British colonies, the flag of Australia was derived from the Blue Ensign. It was adopted in 1901, the year that Australia gained its independence, and the elements of the flag emphasize the ties between Australia and Britain. The Union Jack appears in the canton, with a seven-pointed star – known as the Commonwealth Star – beneath. The seven points represent the six states and the territories (their flags are shown on the following page). In the fly are the five stars of the constellation of the Southern Cross; all are white, and four have seven points, with the smallest having five. The Aboriginal peoples also have a flag to represent them, appearing as two horizontal bands of black (for the people) over red (signifying both the land and the blood shed since the coming of the Europeans), and a gold disc, or sun, in the center over both.

New South Wales

Queensland

South Australia

Tasmania

Victoria

Western Australia

Norfolk Island

Northern Territory

# AUSTRIA, Republic of

©FLAG RATIO 2:3

The triband of red, white and red has been used as the Austrian flag since the Battle of Acre in 1191 when, according to legend, the white tunic of Luitpold V of Babenberg was so bloodstained that the only part which remained white was that which had been under his sword belt. The state flag carries the arms of the Republic, a black imperial eagle, in its center, extending into both red bands. A double-headed eagle had been used on the banner of the Hapsburgs' Austro-Hungarian Empire, but it was modified to have only one head after the empire disintegrated at the end of the First World War. The eagle bears a hammer and sickle and has a three-turreted crown, representing industry, agriculture and commerce. The flag was not used after the Anschluss, or unification with Nazi Germany, in 1938, but when independence was restored in 1945, broken chains were added to the eagle's feet to symbolize Austria's liberty.

# AZERBAIDZHAN, Republic of

FLAG RATIO 1:2

Azerbaidzhan's blue, red and green tricolor was
adopted in early 1991, before the official break-up of
the Union of Soviet Socialist Republics, of which the
country was formerly a part. The meaning attached to
the flag's colors is as follows: blue represents
Azerbaidzhani ethnic affinity with the Turkic peoples
(who use this color in their flags); red symbolizes the
development of culture in Azerbaidzhan; and green
is for the Muslim religion. As do many other states
where the majority of the people are Muslims,
Azerbaidzhan uses the familiar Islamic crescent and
star symbols on its flag, and the star's eight points
rep-resent the eight groupings within the Turkic peoples. The flag was adopted originally in 1918 and was
the national flag until Bolshevik forces occupied the
country in 1920.

# BAHAMAS,
## Commonwealth of the

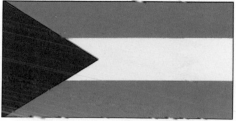

FLAG RATIO 1:2

Now a member of the British Commonwealth, the Bahamas were formerly a British colony, gaining both independence and a new national flag in 1973. The flag's design was based on the winning entry in a competition and represents the qualities of the islands and their people: the aquamarine blue, yellow and aquamarine blue bands symbolize the islands' physical location and attributes, as sandy islands in an archipelago, surrounded by water. The black triangle in the hoist reflects the unity and vigor of the people.

# BAHRAIN, State of

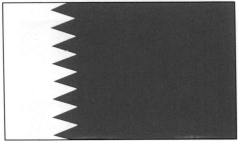

FLAG RATIO 3:5

Bahrain, an archipelago in the Persian Gulf, was under British protection from 1820 to 1971, when independence was attained. Red and white have been the colors of the region since the early 19th century. Red had been the color of the Kharijite Muslims living in eastern Arabia and, in the General Maritime Treaty of 1820, Britain asked all friendly states in the area to display white in their flags (piracy was a problem in the Gulf, and Britain was keen to protect its Arabian and Asian shipping routes). The flag's present form dates from 1932, when the serrated edge was added between the colors, for distinction. The addition was confirmed officially the following year.

# BANGLADESH, People's Republic of

FLAG RATIO 3:5

The Bangladeshi national flag was adopted in 1971, when the country (formerly East Pakistan) gained its independence from West Pakistan. The green of the field represents the fertility of the land and the youth and vigor of the country, as well as reflecting the importance of the Islamic religion. The red circle symbolizes the national struggle for freedom, being the sun of independence rising after the dark night of a bloody struggle. A map of the country initially appeared in the circle, but this was dropped within a few months. The red circle, while seeming to be in the center, is actually set slightly towards the hoist so that it can be seen more clearly as the flag flutters.

# BARBADOS

FLAG RATIO 2:3

Like the flags of other Caribbean nations, the flag of
Barbados emerged after a competition to find a
suitable emblem and, also like others, it emphasizes
the island's favored geographical situation. A triband
of blue, gold, and blue reflects Barbados's position –
and its golden sands – in the blue waters of the
Caribbean. The trident of the sea god, Neptune, was a
symbol used in the colonial arms, so the broken-
shafted version which appears in the gold symbolizes
both the island's break with the past and the continu-
ity of some of its traditions, as well as Barbados's status as an independent nation after its attaining of
independence from Britain in 1966.

# BELARUS, Republic of

FLAG RATIO 1:2

The white, red and white triband of Belarus is based
on the region's old flag and was readopted in 1991
just prior to the official break-up of the Union of
Soviet Socialist Republics, of which the republic had
been a part.

# BELGIUM, Kingdom of

FLAG RATIO 13:15

The colors of the Belgian flag were first used in 1789, a year of revolutionary unrest in Europe, when Belgium, a part of the Austro-Hungarian Empire, fought to free itself from Hapsburg rule. The colors were said to derive from the arms of the province of Brabant, one of the foremost provinces, although the same colors feature in the arms of most of the Belgian provinces. The colors appeared in horizontal bands until 1830, when the country finally became independent, and they were rearranged vertically in a style following that of the French tricolor, although retaining the almost square shape in which the flag had been carried into battle against the Dutch in 1830.

38

# BELIZE

FLAG RATIO 2:3

Formerly the crown colony of British Honduras,
Belize adopted an unofficial flag when it became self-
governing in 1964, and the modern-day flag, which
officially became the national flag on independence
in 1981, is very similar to that. The national arms in
the center date from the early 19th century but were
not officially recognized until 1907. The shield's two
top panels show tools traditionally used in logging,
then the country's main industry. Below these is a
sailing ship, representing trade. The supporters are a
Mestizo and a Creole worker, and above is a mahogany
tree, the national tree representing the main natural
resource. Below all is the motto Sub Umbra Floreo
(I Flourish in the Shade). This version of the flag was
associated particularly with the People's United Party,
so as a counterbalance two bands of red, main color
of the rival United Democratic Party, were added.

# BENIN, Republic of

FLAG RATIO 2:3

Dahomey, as Benin was previously known, was a
colony of France and, in common with many other
African states, adopted the red, yellow, and green
colors of the Pan-African movement, expressive of
African unity and nationalism, on independence in
1960. The colors were adapted to two horizontal
bands of yellow over red, with a green band in the
hoist. The flag was changed in 1975 under the
Communist government (when the country's name
also changed, to Benin) to a plain green field with a
red Communist star in the canton, but with the
collapse of single-party rule in August 1991, the flag
was changed back again to its original design.

# BERMUDA, Colony of

FLAG RATIO 12

One of the oldest of Britain's colonies, Bermuda was
first settled in 1609 after British ships, led by Sir
George Somers's *Sea Venture*, were wrecked off the
coast on their way to Virginia (this event, incidentally,
may have been the inspiration for Shakespeare's *The
Tempest*, written in 1611). A shield for the island coat of
arms was drawn up shortly afterwards, and this can
be seen on the flag today. In the fly of the Red Ensign
– Bermuda was the only British colony to adopt the
Red, rather than Blue Ensign for use on land – is the
island arms: a red lion holds a shield in which is a
depiction of the *Sea Venture* foundering on rocks off
the coast. This flag and shield were officially adopted
in 1910, when the island celebrated its 300th
anniversary of colonial status.

# BHUTAN, Kingdom of

FLAG RATIO 2:3

The design of the flag of Bhutan was adopted in the 1960s, when the country became a member state of the United Nations. Bhutan's name in the local Tibetan dialect is Druk Yil, meaning "Land of the Dragon." Coincidentally, *druk* also means "thunder", thus explaining the local myth that the noise of thunder in the Himalayas to the north was the roaring of dragons among the peaks. Bhutan's dragon represents the nation, although the dragon is also a symbol throughout the Orient of benevolence and power. The two colors on the flag, divided diagonally, represent temporal and spiritual power: the lower portion, flame-red, stands for Buddhist spiritual authority, while the upper portion of saffron represents royal authority.

# BOLIVIA, Republic of

FLAG RATIO 2:3

The colors of this flag are symbolic, and were adopted by Bolivia in 1825–26 after the country had gained independence. The horizontal design of the tricolor dates from 1851. Red stands for both national valor and the blood shed in the struggle for independence; yellow symbolizes the mineral resources of the country; and green represents its agricultural wealth. The addition of national arms to the center of the civil flag gives the state flag: a blue disc, centered on the yellow band, contains an oval, inside which is a scene representing the country's natural, mineral and agricultural riches. The oval's border bears the country's name and nine stars, representing Bolivia's nine provinces. Above is a condor, the national bird, and surrounding it are arms and the national colors, together with laurel wreaths and a cap of liberty.

# BOSNIA-HERZEGOVINA, Republic of

FLAG RATIO 1:2

The flag chosen in 1992 to represent the newly independent state of Bosnia-Herzegovina bears the arms of the last royal ruler of the state, King Stephen Tvrtko (1376–91). The source of the fleurs-de-lys on the shield is not certain: they may be French in origin, as the Anjou dynasty once ruled neighboring Hungary, and Tvrtko claimed to be related to the Hungarian royal family. It is more likely that they represent a lily which grows in Bosnia. The flag lacks any reference to more recent history, which saw the country's domination by the Turkish Ottoman Empire (15th–19th centuries) or by Yugoslavia (up to 1992). With its white field and neutral central emblem, the adoption of this flag may have been a deliberate attempt to find a design which would appeal to all the ethnic groups – Bosnian Muslims, Croats and Serbs – in this divided country.

# BOTSWANA, Republic of

FLAG RATIO 2:3

The national flag of Botswana was adopted when the protectorate gained its independence from Britain in 1966. It comprises a horizontal black stripe, fimbriated in white, across a blue field. The colors on the flag correspond to those on the national coat of arms. The blue represents water, of vital importance in this largely arid land whose main industries are animal husbandry and agriculture (the motto on the national arms is Pula, meaning, "Let there be rain"). The white–black–white bands depict the racial harmony of the people as well as the pluralist nature of society. They are inspired by the coat of the zebra, the national animal.

# BRAZIL, Federative Republic of

FLAG RATIO 7:10

The colors of this flag have been in use since 1822 when the Crown Prince of Portugal, who fled Europe in 1807 to escape Napoleon, declared Brazil independent. The green field signifies Brazil's rain forests and the yellow central diamond its mineral resources, in particular its gold. The central sphere depicts the constellations of stars in the night sky over Rio de Janeiro. The stars represent the Brazilian states and Federal District. The central band bears the words Ordem e Progresso (Order and Progress), and the whole emblem replaces the royal coat of arms which were dropped in 1889, when the monarchy was overthrown. The idea for the use of a globe may have come from earlier flags which included a crowned armillary sphere, an instrument used by early navigators as well as being the personal symbol of the Portuguese King Manuel I.

46

# BRUNEI DARUSSALAM

FLAG RATIO 1:2

The flag of Brunei has evolved gradually throughout this century. Its base, a plain yellow field, was the flag of the Sultan, its ruler. To this were added in 1906 two diagonal stripes, a broad one of white over a narrower of black, in recognition of British protection. The state arms were added in 1959. A crescent, a traditional symbol of Islam, bears words meaning, "Always Give Service by God's Guidance." The motto below reads, "Brunei, City of Peace." The arms on either side are upraised to God.

# BULGARIA, Republic of

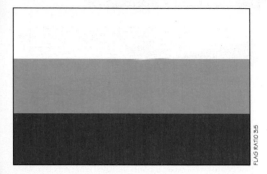

FLAG RATIO 3:5

The colors of the Bulgarian flag are both symbolic in themselves and representative of the Pan-Slav nationalist movement of the 19th century. As the Slav communities of Eastern Europe tried to pull away from the Hapsburg Empire in the middle years of the century, so they fell under the influence of imperial Russia, and the Pan-Slav flags tended to use the Russian white, blue, and red tricolor as a model. However, green was used in place of blue in the Bulgarian flag, designed in 1878, both to distinguish it from the Russian and Slovenian flags, which were identical, and to express the youthfulness of the emergent nation. White is said to represent a love of peace, and red symbolizes the valor of the people.

# BURKINA, People's Democratic Republic of

FLAG RATIO 2:3

Burkina was a colony of France from the end of the First World War until 1960, taking the name of Upper Volta on independence. Its name was derived from the river whose source lay within its borders, and the colors from the names of the river's tributaries – Black Volta, White Volta and Red Volta – were given to the horizontal tricolor which was adopted as the national flag. However, both the name of the country and the flag were changed in 1984 in what was intended to be a deliberate turning away from the colonial past and an identification with the concerns of its own continent. The colors of the Pan-African movement, representing aspirations towards African unity, were adopted: two bands of red over green, with yellow in the form of a central star.

# BURUNDI, Republic of

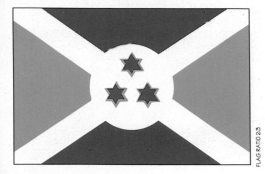

FLAG RATIO 2:3

As with so many former colonies, the flag of Burundi celebrates the country's achievement of independence. Its basic component, a white saltire, does not represent any martyr or saint, but its white color is expressive of a desire for peace. Its top and bottom quarters, of red, commemorate the struggle for independence, first from Germany and then from Belgium. Its green quarters, at the hoist and the fly, are expressive of hope for the future, while the three red stars fimbriated in green, in the white circle, represent the three words of the national motto: Unity Work Progress. The flag was first adopted on independence in 1962, with a plant and a drum in the center, symbolic of the then ruling family. The flag took on its present design in 1967 with the overthrow of the monarchy.

# CAMBODIA, State of

The flag of Cambodia has always featured a representation of the 12th-century Angkor Wat temple, the country's most famous monument, although the colors in the field have varied slightly. The United Nations supervised the settlement of the country's civil war and it is now a constitutional monarchy. The latest form of its flag, which is particularly associated with the new king, Prince Sihanouk, was introduced in June 1993. This flag was originally introduced in 1948 and was used up to the founding of the Khmer Republic in 1970.

# CAMEROON, Republic of

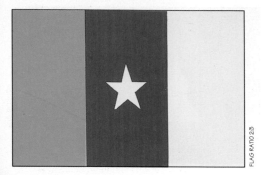

FLAG RATIO 2:3

The Pan-African colors – representing aspirations towards African unity – arranged in the style of the French tricolor, form the basis of the flag of Cameroon. Until 1960–61, the country was split into two parts, administered by France and Britain. The French part was the first to achieve independence in 1960, and the tricolor had been used as a model for the green, red and yellow flag which had been adopted three years before. When the British sector joined the rest the following year, two vertically arranged yellow stars were added to the canton to reflect the two parts of the country. In 1972 these were replaced by a single yellow star in the center, representing national unity.

# CANADA

FLAG RATIO 1:2

The distinctive red and white flag of Canada was
adopted in 1965 after efforts to find an emblem which
would be acceptable to all citizens. The Red Ensign,
with the Canadian arms in the fly, was in use from
1892 to 1921, when the arms were updated. The flag
remained unpopular with many, particularly the
French community. Red and white, as used in the
Canadian Red Ensign and in the coat of arms, were
the national colors, and they were used in the new
flag: a white, full-depth central square with a red
band down either side. In the white square is a large
red maple leaf, a Canadian emblem from the 18th
century. Each of the provinces and territories also has
its own flag (see the following pages).

*Alberta*

*British Columbia*

*Manitoba*

*New Brunswick*

54

*Newfoundland*

*Nova Scotia*

*Ontario*

*Prince Edward Island*

*Quebec*

*Saskatchewan*

*Northwest Territories*

*Yukon*

# CAPE VERDE, Republic of

FLAG RATIO 2:3

The adoption of a new constitution in 1992 resulted in a completely new design for the Cape Verde flag. The country originally gained its independence from Portugal in 1975 and its flag was modelled on that of Guinea-Bissau; a planned federation of the two countries was cancelled after a coup in Guinea-Bissau in 1980. As in many former African colonies, the green, red, and yellow of the Pan-African movement were used in its flag, but the break with Guinea-Bissau and a move away from a one-party system in the country has led to a dropping of the old colors. The new flag has ten stars representing the ten islands which comprise the country, while the blue field stands for the sea, and the horizontal stripes denote the islands' location.

# CAYMAN ISLANDS, Colony of the

FLAG RATIO 1:2

Discovered by Columbus in 1503, the Cayman Islands were first called "Tortugas" after the great number of turtles found there. The islands were colonized by Britain, and were administered by Jamaica until 1962, when they reverted to their status as a British colony. The basic flag is the Blue Ensign, with the islands' coat of arms, granted in 1958, set in a white disc in the fly. A shield bears an English heraldic lion against a red background in the chief (top part), with blue and white wavy lines below, to represent the sea, and three yellow-fimbriated green stars superimposed on the waves, representing the three islands that comprise the group: Grand Cayman, Little Cayman, and Cayman Brac. Above the shield is a pineapple, representing the islands' connection with Jamaica, and a turtle above a coil of rope, which the islands manufactured and exported at the beginning of this century. Below a scroll bears the motto, "He hath founded it upon the seas".

# CENTRAL AFRICAN REPUBLIC

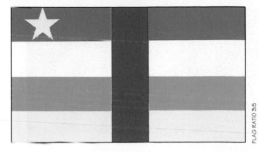

FLAG RATIO 3:5

The desire for harmony and cooperation between the Central African Republic and its former colonizer, France, as well as for African unity, is expressed in the unusual design of this flag which was adopted in 1958, two years before the country gained its independence Its colors symbolize desirable qualities, including freedom (blue), equality and purity (white), hope (green), and tolerance (yellow). The red is representative both of national heroes and of unity, crossing the other four colors. Both the colors of France and the colors of the Pan-African movement, with its ultimate ideal of African unity, are present. The five-pointed gold star in the blue of the canton expresses further the hope of African unity.

# CHAD, Republic of

FLAG RATIO 2:3

The flag of the Republic of Chad, adopted the year before the country became independent of France in 1960, is based on the tricolor of France, with the substitution of yellow for white in the middle, thus containing two of the French colors and two of the colors from the Pan-African movement for African unity. The colors also carry their own significance: blue is said to symbolize the sky and the waters of the south, yellow the sun and the deserts of the north, and red valor and the national sacrifice in the struggle for freedom.

# CHILE, Republic of

FLAG RATIO 2:3

While the French flag was used as a model by many countries in Europe who wanted to stress the ideals of progress and revolution, so too was the American flag in the New World in the early part of the 19th century. The colors of the Chilean flag were based on the Stars and Stripes, and it was adopted in 1817 during the struggle for freedom from Spain, initially being a horizontal tricolor of blue, white, and red. The design was modified in 1854 to the present configuration: two horizontal bands of white over red, with a blue canton charged with a white star. The white band depicts the snow of the Andes Mountains, the blue the sky, the red the blood of the patriots who died in the struggle for independence, and the white star is a symbol of progress.

# CHINA, People's Republic of

FLAG RATIO 2:3

The five-star red flag of the People's Republic of China was officially adopted in 1949 on the same day as the Republic itself came into being. The flag's field of red uses the color traditionally associated with both China and revolution. The large gold star in the canton represents the Common Program of the Communist Party, while the four smaller stars symbolize the social classes it unites: the workers, the peasants, the petty bourgeois and the capitalists sympathetic to the Party. Collectively, the five stars symbolize the unity of the people under the Communist Party. The flags used by the Kuomintang (Chinese Nationalist Party) government from the early part of the 20th century until the establishment of the People's Republic, are now used in Taiwan (see China, Republic of).

# CHINA, Republic of

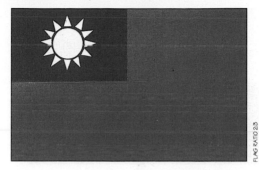

FLAG RATIO 2:3

The island of Taiwan, or Formosa as it was then known, became home to the Kuomintang, the Chinese Nationalist Party, after their defeat on the Chinese mainland by the Communist forces of Mao Tse Tung in 1949. The flag they brought had been adopted as the national flag of China from 1928–49, while the nationalists had formed the government, although it had been in use as the Kuomintang party flag from 1914, shortly after the overthrow of the imperial dynasty. The 12-rayed sun symbolizes unceasing progress, each ray representing two hours of the day, while the three colors each represent desirable qualities, including purity, equality, and selfless sacrifice.

# COLOMBIA, Republic of

FLAG RATIO 2:3

This flag, like those of Colombia's neighbors, Ecuador and Venezuela, is based on that flown by the armies of Simón Bolívar during his rebellion against Spanish rule. The flag was originally used by Bolívar's predecessor, Francisco de Miranda, in his fight against Spanish rule in 1806. The flag continued to be used by Colombia even after Ecuador and Venezuela finally broke away from what was then Gran Colombia in 1830. Today, the colors are said to represent the following: yellow or gold, for Colombia's natural riches; blue, for the sky and seas surrounding Colombia; and red, for the blood shed by the freedom fighters during the struggle for independence from Spain.

# COMOROS, Federal Islamic Republic of the

FLAG RATIO 3:5

Unlike many former French territories, the islands of the Comoros archipelago did not use the tricolor as a basis for their flag after independence in 1975. Instead, both the crescent and the green color of the field represent the main religion, Islam, a legacy of much earlier and more lengthy conquests by Arabs. The flag was adopted in 1978 and its four stars represent the four principal islands of the group: Grande Comore, Anjouan, Moliéli, and Mayotte, even though the latter voted to remain a French dependency in 1975 and is not part of the Federal Islamic Republic.

# CONGO, Republic of the

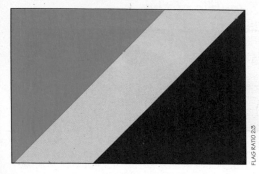

FLAG RATIO 2:3

The original flag of the Congo was officially restored as the national flag in 1991 after 21 years of disuse. The green, yellow and red diagonal design had been used from the winning of independence from France in 1960, to the establishment of the People's Republic in 1970. In the intervening years the flag had been one which was modelled on the Hammer and Sickle of the old Union of Soviet Socialist Republics, with local tools representing the importance of industry and agriculture. The colors of both original and Communist flags were the same, and are expressive of solidarity with the ideals of the Pan-African movement for African unity.

# COOK ISLANDS

FLAG RATIO 1:2

These islands were named after Captain James Cook,
although they were discovered almost 200 years before
he visited them in the late 18th century. They were
administered by New Zealand from 1901–65, when
they became a self-governing dependency. The basis
of the islands' flag is the Blue Ensign, emphasizing
indirectly their links with the Commonwealth
through New Zealand. In the fly is a ring of 15 five-
pointed stars, representing the 15 islands in the group.
The choice of stars as a design feature is something
which the Cook Islands have in common with other
Pacific island countries. The flag has been in use since
1979.

# COSTA RICA, Republic of

FLAG RATIO 3:5

Costa Rica's membership in the United Provinces of Central America (1823–38) is reflected in the colors and composition of its flag which, like those of the other federation members (El Salvador, Guatemala, Honduras and Nicaragua), is modelled on the Argentinian blue–white–blue triband. It was adopted on independence in 1821, the red stripe being added in 1848 when Costa Rica became a republic, both as a distinguishing feature and to reflect the colors of France which was then in the grasp of revolutionary fervor. The addition of the national arms in a white oval, set in the red band towards the hoist, forms the state flag. They depict two sailing ships on two seas (the Pacific and the Caribbean) separated by Costa Rica, itself represented by three mountains – the volcanoes Barba, Irazú and Poás. A rising sun signals the dawning of a new era, while seven stars above it represent the provinces of the country. The words America Central, set above, recall the old federation.

# CROATIA, Republic of

FLAG RATIO 1:2

Together with other Slavic states of the Hapsburg Empire, Croatia was involved in the Pan-Slav movement in the 18th and 19th centuries. In 1848 attempts to secure a measure of self-determination resulted in the fostering of Russian goodwill, and almost all the Slav states adopted flags based on Russia's tricolor, the Croatian red, white and blue tricolor being a variant on this. The southern Slav states (Croatia, Bosnia, Herzegovina, Montenegro, Slovenia and Serbia) were joined in a new nation in 1918, using the same basic tricolor which is still the Yugoslavian flag. Traditional rivalries between the constituent states remained, and with the stabilizing force of Communism gone by the late 1980s, Yugoslavia broke up, Croatia and Slovenia leaving the union in 1992. Croatia has readopted as its flag the traditional tricolor, with the national arms in the center: a shield of red and silver squares surmounted by a crown as in the traditional arms of Croatia Ancient, Dubrovnik, Dalmatia, Istria, and Slavonia.

# CUBA, Republic of

The flag of Cuba, designed in 1849, was influenced in design and color by the flags of the United States of America and France, then regarded as revolutionary in outlook and aspiration, particularly as the latter was a prime mover in the revolutionary fervor which was sweeping Europe at that time. The three horizontal blue stripes represent the three provinces of Cuba which existed in the mid 19th century, and the two white stripes show the purity of Cuban ideals. The red triangle in the hoist is a symbol of the bloodshed and sacrifice of the people struggling to gain their independence from the Spanish Empire, while the white star indicates Cuba's status as a free and independent nation. The flag was adopted by the independence movement of 1868–69, and was retained as the national flag after independence was achieved fully in 1902.

# CYPRUS, Republic of

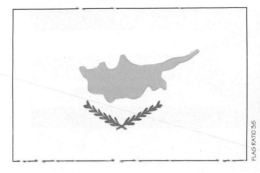

FLAG RATIO 3:5

In view of the hostilities which took place after its adoption, the Cypriot flag is a poignant symbol of well-intentioned attempts to unite the Greek and Turkish communities on the island. The use of blue and red, colors associated with Greece and Turkey, was deliberately avoided. The adoption of both the white field and crossed olive branches is symbolic of a desire for peace between the communities, white also being a neutral color between the two. A map of Cyprus appears in orange, recalling the rich copper deposits for which the island was famous in ancient times. The flag came into use when the island became independent from Britain in 1960, and it may be flown together with the Greek and Turkish flags on public holidays.

# CZECH REPUBLIC

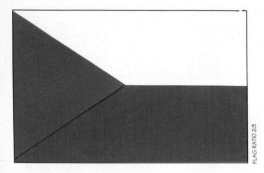

FLAG RATIO 2:3

The flag which was Czechoslovakia's has been in use since 1920, two years after the state came into being with the collapse of the Austro-Hungarian Empire. As it was formed mainly of three states – Bohemia, Slovakia and Moravia – a flag was needed which combined elements and colors of all three to foster national unity. Bohemia's white-over-red flag forms the basis, with the blue triangle in the hoist representing the blue of Slovakia. The flag was abolished by the Nazis, who invaded Czechoslovakia in 1938, but was re-adopted after liberation in 1945. Although the Czechs and Slovaks had been involved in the Pan-Slav movement for home rule from the Hapsburg Empire, the adoption of the red, white and blue symbolic of the movement was, in this case, coincidental. When the country split in two in 1992, the Czechs kept the traditional flag, while Slovakia adopted a new design.

# DENMARK, Kingdom of

FLAG RATIO 28:34

The flag of Denmark, the Dannebrog, may have been in continual use for longer than any other national flag. According to legend, the white cross on a red field was given as a sign from Heaven to the crusader King Valdemar II of Denmark before the Battle of Lyndaniz against the pagan Estonians, in 1219. The distinctive off-center cross, with the extended arm in the fly, was subsequently used as a model by the other Scandinavian countries, several of whom were ruled from Denmark for centuries. The plain flag shown above is the civic flag, but cut into a swallow-tail shape it becomes the state flag and naval ensign.

# DJIBOUTI, Republic of

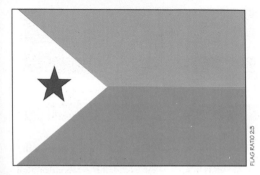

FLAG RATIO 2:3

1977 was the year in which Djibouti (formerly French Somaliland) won its independence from France, and its new flag was based on the flag of the Ligue Populaire pour L'Indépendence (People's League for Independence), who had been the leaders in the independence struggle. The party had used the same basic flag since 1972. The two horizontal bands of blue over green represent the peoples of the country: blue for the Issas, who are Somalis (Somalia has a light blue flag), and green for the Afars, who are Muslims (green being a color traditionally used to represent Islam). The white triangle in the hoist symbolizes equality and peace, while the five-pointed red star centered in the triangle stands for national unity.

# DOMINICA, Commonweath of

FLAG RATIO 1:2

The sisserou parrot, which stands in the center of the national flag of Dominica, is the country's national bird and is unique to the island; it is symbolic of high national aspirations. It is surrounded by 10 green stars, which stand for the island's 10 parishes. The parrot and stars are set in a red roundel which signifies the national commitment to social justice. The central motif appears on a cross of yellow, black and white, the three strands representing the Holy Trinity, while the colors themselves represent: sunshine, agriculture and the native peoples of the island (yellow); the purity of the people's aspirations, and of local water (white); and the soil and the people's African heritage (black). The flag's field is green, symbolizing the lush vegetation of the island. The whole flag echoes Dominica's motto, Après Bondie C'est La Ter (After the Good Lord Comes the Land).

# DOMINICAN REPUBLIC

FLAG RATIO 2:3

The Dominican Republic occupies the eastern part of the Caribbean island of Hispaniola which it shares with Haiti, once an invader. The flag reflects the islanders' struggle to free themselves from Haitian occupation, with the white cross of liberty superimposed on the blue and red of the Haitian flag (the blue and red in the fly were subsequently transposed). The flag was adopted on independence in 1844. Red now symbolizes the blood and suffering of the original freedom fighters, blue represents liberty, and the white cross stands for the sacrifices of the people. The state flag carries the national arms in the center: a shield of the state colors contains a gold cross and an open Bible. The shield is surrounded by palm and laurel branches, and a scroll at the top reads Dios, Patria, Libertad (God, Country, Liberty), the motto of the freedom fighters of the 1840s.

# ECUADOR, Republic of

Like the flags of Colombia and Venezuela, that of
Ecuador is based on the flag of Francisco de Miranda
and Simón Bolívar, whose independence movement
was responsible for liberating South America from
the rule of imperial Spain. Ecuador was united with
Colombia and Venezuela in Gran Colombia in 1822,
but Ecuador left the federation eight years later. It was
ultimately decided that the same colors as the
Colombian flag should be retained. The addition of
the arms to the center of the basic civil flag gives the
state flag. The arms depict a scene with Mount
Chimborazo, the highest mountain in the country, in
the background, and a ship on a river in the
foreground, symbolizing trade. A yellow sun of independence is surrounded by four zodiac signs
representing the months March–June of 1845, when
Ecuador successfully defended its independence. A
South American condor above symbolizes freedom,
while an axe and fasces below represent the authority
of the republic.

# EGYPT, Arab Republic of

FLAG RATIO 2:3

In common with many of its Near-Eastern neighbors, Egypt's flag is based on the colors of the Pan-Arab movement, which aimed at securing independence for the Arab peoples from the Ottoman Empire in the first part of this century. Britain had occupied the country from 1882–1914. In 1952 the monarchy was overthrown, and the following year a republic was declared. In 1958 Egypt and Syria formed the United Arab Republic, which lasted for three years. The flag they adopted was like Syria's present-day one, but in 1972, when the Federation of Arab Republics, comprising Egypt, Syria and Libya, came into being, the two stars were replaced by the national arms. In the version today, these comprise an eagle, said to be the emblem of Saladin (the 12th-century sultan and opponent of the Crusaders), bearing on its breast a shield with the national colors.

# EL SALVADOR, Republic of

FLAG RATIO 3:5

The El Salvadorean flag, officially adopted in 1912, is similar in color and design to the flags of Costa Rica, Guatemala, Honduras and Nicaragua, all former members of the United Provinces of Central America, which took the Argentinian flag as a model for their own. Three versions of the flag are in use: plain, for the civil flag, with the addition of the words Dios, Union, Libertad (God, Unity, Liberty) across the white band for the merchant flag, and with the arms in the center of the white band for the state flag and ensign. The arms comprise an equilateral triangle, signifying liberty, equality and fraternity, and containing a scene showing five mountains (the five federation members) between two seas, with a red cap of liberty set above, and in front of a shining sun. Around it is the date September 15, 1821, to mark the country's liberation from Spain, and a rainbow sits just under the apex of the triangle. The national colors are ranged behind, with a scroll bearing the national motto below.

# EQUATORIAL GUINEA, Republic of

FLAG RATIO 5:8

A former Spanish colony which gained independence in 1968, Equatorial Guinea's flags reflect the ideals and physical characteristics of the country. The flag, also adopted in 1968, comprises a tricolor with horizontal bands of green, white and red, symbolizing agriculture, peace and independence respectively. The blue triangle in the hoist represents the sea, which both divides the mainland from and links it to the country's five offshore islands. The addition of the arms to the center of the white band gives the state flag: a shield containing the depiction of the indigenous silk cotton tree is topped by six gold stars, representing the mainland and five islands. The national motto, Unidad, Paz, Justicia, (Unity, Peace, Justice), appears on a scroll below.

# ERITREA

FLAG RATIO 2:3

Eritrea gained its freedom in May 1993 after the collapse of the Communist regime in Ethiopia. It had been an automomous province of Ethiopia, with its own flag, until 1959, and the old flag, together with the flag of the Eritrean People's Liberation Front, has been used as the basis for the new. The olive wreath and stem are features from the old flag, themselves originally inspired by the flag of the United Nations. The rest of the flag is derived from the Eritrean People's Liberation Front flag, with the olive wreath replacing the yellow star previously appearing in the red triangle.

# ESTONIA, Republic of

FLAG RATIO 7:11

The tricolor of Estonia was first used in 1881 during popular uprisings against the occupying Russian Tsarist forces. Use of the flag was frowned upon by the Russians, but after the break-up of the Tsarist empire in 1917 Estonia enjoyed a period of freedom during which the blue, black and white tricolor was adopted as the national flag. It was suppressed again after the invasion by Stalinist forces in 1940 but was readopted officially as the republic's flag in 1990, over a year before the disintegration of the Union of Soviet Socialist Republics. The blue stands for the sky, and the mutual fidelity of the Estonian peoples; black for the soil and the Estonians' mythological ancestors; and white for the peoples' wish for freedom, and for the snow which covers this Baltic country for six months in every year.

# ETHIOPIA

The flag of Ethiopia is probably one of the most influential in the world, as it was taken as one of the models for the Pan-African colors of African unity which were adopted by so many emergent African nations in the 20th century. Ethiopia was one of the first two independent African states of modern times (Liberia being the other) and gained prominence and influence on the continent after the election as emperor of Ras Tafari. The colors were in use in the 1890s, when the country successfully resisted invasion by Italy; then, they were flown in the form of three separate pennants, one below the other. The colors may have been used because of their symbolizm in Coptic Christianity, being representative of both the Holy Trinity and the three virtues of Faith, Hope and Charity.

# FALKLAND ISLANDS,
## Colony of the

FLAG RATIO 1:2

Together with South Georgia and the South
Sandwich Islands, the Falkland Islands are a British
territory. The islands were discovered in 1592, and
over the centuries have been claimed by several
countries including, at various times, France, Spain
and Argentina as well as Britain. The flag flown today
is the Blue Ensign with the islands' arms appearing in
a white disc in the fly. In the shield are a sheep standing on an island, depicting the islands' main econom-
ic resource, and below blue and white wavy lines
representing the sea, with a sailing ship, the *Desire*, on
the waves. The scroll below bears the motto, Desire
the Right, a reference to the ship which dis-covered
the islands, and the consequent claiming of them by
Britain.

# FAROES, Faroe Islands

FLAG RATIO 8:11

First settled by Norse people in the 9th century, then passing to Danish control in 1380 after the union of the Norwegian and Danish crowns, the Faroes have been under Scandinavian influence for centuries, and this is evident in the design of their flag. Although the islands are still a part of the kingdom of Denmark, they have had an autonomous legislature since the mid 1940s, with the flag first being adopted in 1948. The colors of Denmark are reversed out to an off-center red cross on a white field. The cross is fimbriated in blue, possibly a reference to past Norwegian influences.

# FIJI, Republic of

FLAG RATIO 1:2

Ties with the United Kingdom are stressed in the flag of Fiji, a former British colony. The design dates from 1970, when the islands gained their independence, and is based on the Blue Ensign, although with a paler blue in the field. The continuing connection with the United Kingdom is displayed in the Union Jack in the canton, while a modified version of Fiji's state arms is in the fly. The chief, at the top of the shield, displays an English lion holding a cocoa pod. Below this the shield is quartered by the cross of St. George with, in the four corners, a sugar cane plant, a coconut palm, a bunch of bananas (all these being indigenous plants) and a white dove of peace bearing an olive branch.

# FINLAND, Republic of

FLAG RATIO 11:18

The identification of Finland with the Scandinavian nations is reflected clearly in its flag. The country had been conquered by Sweden in the 12th century, but passed into Russian control in 1809. The opportunity for independence was seized in 1917 when Russia was in revolution, and while the national flag was adopted then, its design dated from the mid 19th century. The blue and white represent the Finnish lakes and snow. The state flag has the addition of the national arms in the center of the cross; a red field containing a lion rampant with a mailed arm bearing a sword, and treading on a scimitar, representing national resistance to eastern invaders. Its design dates from the 16th century.

# FRANCE, French Republic

FLAG RATIO 2:3

The colors and philosophy of design of the flag of the French Republic have made it not only instantly recognizable, but probably the most influential flag in the world. Since its adoption in 1794, the tricolor design or its colors or both, have been used by revolutionary movements the world over to represent the spirit of their cause, with the successful ones, such as the Irish revolutionaries and the Indian National Congress, subsequently using it as a model for their own national flags. The colors are understood to be the blue and red of Paris, combined with the white of the Bourbon monarchy, although they have other associations dating as far back as the reign of Charlemagne (c.742–814). The austere 1794 design, intended to be a radical departure from many of the more fussy contemporary flags, was meant to symbolize the new republican principles.

# GABON, *Gabonese Republic*

FLAG RATIO 3:4

Once a part of France's African empire, Gabon gained its independence in 1960. However, the influence of the French tricolor can be seen in the design of its flag, which is a horizontal tricolor of green, yellow and blue, a combination of the French and Pan-African colors of African unity. The green represents the country's rainforests and the lumber industry, the source of much of the nation's wealth; the yellow represents the sun; and the blue stands for the sea. A former design, dropped just before independence, had a narrower yellow band and a French tricolor in the canton.

# GAMBIA, Republic of the

FLAG RATIO 2:3

Gambia, the smallest African country, was a colony of Britain from 1843 until it gained its independence in 1965. The new national flag was adopted at this time. It has three broad bands of red, blue and green, separated by two fimbriations of white. The green is symbolic of the land, while the blue represents the Gambia River flowing over it, and the red stands for the hot sun beating down on both.

# GEORGIA, Republic of

FLAG RATIO 3:5

The new flag of Georgia is essentially no different from that used in the region during its last period of independence. The crimson of the field represents both the bright past of Georgia, and joy. The black of the canton's bicolor symbolizes the period which Georgia spent under Russian control, while the white stands for the nation's peaceful development, and hope. The flag was first adopted officially in 1918, then again in 1990, a year before the official break-up of the Union of Soviet Socialist Republics, of which Georgia had been a part.

# GERMANY, Federal Republic of

FLAG RATIO 3:5

Black and gold were colors associated with the first German Empire which collapsed in 1806, and they were used together with the red from the uniforms of soldiers who fought in campaigns against Napoleon. The colors, arranged horizontally in a tricolor, were used as a rallying banner by those seeking unification of the German states. The tricolor was first adopted in 1848, the year of revolutions in Europe, but the process of unification suffered setbacks, and the flag was not officially sanctioned after 1849. The black, white and red of Prussia was the first flag of a united Germany, but in 1919 the black, red and gold tricolor was readopted by the Weimar government. It was abolished by Adolf Hitler when he came to power in 1933, being officially readopted only in 1949. The state flag carries arms of a black eagle on a gold shield, set slightly towards the hoist. All the provinces of Germany have their own flags.

# GHANA, *Republic of*

FLAG RATIO 2:3

Ghana was the first of the liberated African nations to
take as its colors those of Ethiopia and the Pan-
African movement of African unity. The colors of this
flag, however, are also symbolic in themselves: red is
taken to represent the blood of the freedom fighters
who died for independence, yellow is the mineral
wealth of the country (when a British colony, Ghana
was known as the Gold Coast), and green is the rich
forests. The black, five-pointed star set in the center of
the yellow band represents the lodestar of African
freedom. The Ghanaian flag was seminal in its influence on the subsequent adoption of flags by former
African colonies throughout the 1960s.

# GIBRALTAR, Colony of

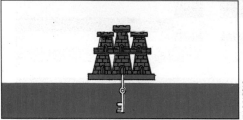

FLAG RATIO 1:2

Gibraltar was one of the ancient Pillars of Hercules which delimited the known world to Europeans. It was ceded to Britain by Spain after the Treaty of Utrecht in 1713 and, while largely self-governing, remains the last British colony on mainland Europe. Consequently, the official flag is the Union Jack, although the white and red flag has been in use unofficially by citizens there since 1966. It is based on the city arms presented to Gibraltar in 1502 by Ferdinand and Isabella of Spain, and features two unequal horizontal bands of white over red. On the white is a three-turretted castle from which hangs a key, symbolizing Gibraltar's strategic importance as the gateway to the Mediterranean.

# GREECE, Hellenic Republic

FLAG RATIO 7:12

The blue and white colors of the Greek flag were first used in the 1820s and '30s, during the country's struggle for independence from the Turkish Ottoman Empire. The nine blue and white stripes are said to represent the national motto, Elentheria a Thanatos (Liberty or Death), which was a battle cry used when fighting the Turks. The white cross on blue in the canton represents Greek Orthodox Christianity. The flag was adopted in its most recent form in 1978, having been used intermittently since independence with another, featuring a blue field with a white cross. This flag is now seen only in an unofficial capacity within the country itself.

# GREENLAND

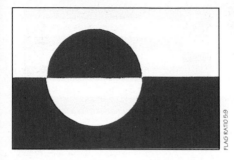

FLAG RATIO 5:9

The largest island in the world, Greenland was discovered by Europeans around 982, although it had been settled up to 3,000 years before then by hunters from North America. Although settled by Norwegians in the 10th century, the island passed to Denmark after the union of the Norse and Danish crowns. From the 18th century until the 1950s, Greenland was run by the Royal Greenland Trading Company, being absorbed then into the Kingdom of Denmark until achieving home rule in 1979. The island remains a self-governing part of the kingdom. Greenland's flag was the winning entry in a locally held competition, and was officially adopted in 1985. The red and white of Denmark have been retained but now depict a far-northern scene, with the white of the flag representing the inland ice and icebergs, and the red the sunrise and sunset.

# GRENADA, State of

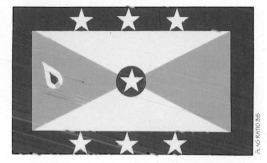

The flag of Grenada was adopted in 1974, on the island's independence from Britain. It is quartered by two diagonals, with two yellow triangles at the top and bottom, and two green triangles, in the hoist and fly. These are surrounded by a red border, with six five-pointed yellow stars distributed along top and bottom, and a seventh contained in a red disc in the center of the diagonals. The seven stars are representative of the island's seven parishes, while the depiction of a nutmeg in the green triangle of the hoist acknowledges the island's main source of wealth. The colors, too, are symbolic: green for agriculture and the land; yellow for the sunshine; and red for freedom and the fervor of the people. Coincidentally or intentionally, these are also the colors of the Pan-African movement for African unity.

# GUAM

FLAG RATIO 21:40

A strategically important island in the Western
Pacific, Guam is a dependency of the United States of
America. It was taken by the USA from Spain in 1898
and is now home to an American naval and air base.
Guam has had a measure of self-government since
1950. Its flag was adopted in 1917, and comprises a
red-bordered blue field with a red-bordered oval in
the center, showing a beach with a palm tree and
small sailing craft, with the island's name in red
capitals. The flag of Guam is flown only in
conjunction with that of the USA.

# GUATEMALA, *Republic of*

Together with Costa Rica, El Salvador, Honduras and Nicaragua, Guatemala made up the complement of five member states of the United Provinces of Central America, who broke away from Spanish rule in 1821. The federation broke up 18 years later, but all five nations have retained the same basic blue, white and blue tribands, originally based on the Argentinian flag. Guatemala changed its bands from a horizontal to a vertical orientation in 1871. The state flag bears the national arms in the center and unlike those of other former federation members, these are not based on the old federation arms. They feature a quetzal bird perched on a scroll bearing the date of national independence, September 15, 1821. Behind these are arms, symbolizing a willingness to defend the country, and a laurel wreath. Guatemala's arms were initially adopted in 1825 and reached their present appearance after several revisions, in 1968.

# GUINEA, Republic of

FLAG RATIO 2/3

The colors of the Pan-African movement and the design and proportions of the French tricolor were the inspirations for Guinea's flag of red, yellow and green vertical bands. Guinea achieved its independence from France in 1958 and, following Ghana's lead of the previous year, adopted the green, yellow and red expressive of African solidarity and a desire for unity. In Guinea's case, the colors also reflect the three words of the national motto, Travail, Justice, Solidarité; work is represented by red, justice by yellow, and solidarity by green. They were also the colors of the Partie Démocratique du Guinea, the dominant political party of the time and responsible for leading the country to independence.

# GUINEA-BISSAU, Republic of

FLAG RATIO 1:2

Guinea-Bissau's flag was adopted in 1973, the same year as the country proclaimed its independence from Portugal. The flag is based on one which had been used by the liberation movement since the early 1960s, which in its turn was probably based on the flag of Ghana, the first of the former African colonies to achieve independence, a few years before. The red, yellow and green are the colors of the Pan-African movement, and the black star also is expressive of a desire for African unity. In the flag of Guinea-Bissau, however, the colors are also symbolic in their own right: red for the blood of the fallen heroes of the independence movement; green for hope; yellow for the sun, the source of life; and the black star for the African continent.

# GUYANA, Co-operative Republic of

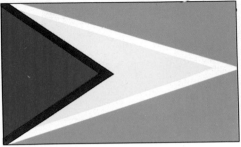

FLAG RATIO 3:5

The striking flag of this former British colony was
designed, as were the flags of so many new and
emergent nations, to reflect the country's physical
attributes and the qualities of its people. The flag has
two triangles pointing out from the hoist – a smaller
red one and a larger gold one spanning the fly,
fimbriated in black and white respectively – on a
green field. The red is said to represent the energy of
the people in the building of the new country, while
the gold symbolizes the mineral wealth and the
country's forward thrust, maintained by perseverance
(black). The white fimbriation symbolizes the
country's rivers, and the green field its agriculture
and forests. The flag was adopted in 1966, the same
year as Guyana achieved its independence.

# HAITI, Republic of

FLAG RATIO 35:44

Two rival flags have been used alternatively as the
national flag since Haiti became independent in 1804.
The most recent change came in 1986 with the fall of
the Duvalier régime, when the original flag of two
bands of blue over red, was readopted. Said to have
been modelled on the French tricolor, it was used
from around 1804, and its colors have subsequently
come to be interpreted as representing the country's
two communities, the blacks (blue) and the mulattoes
(red). The state flag bears the national arms in a white
panel in the center: a palm tree surrounded by
weapons, with the motto l'union fait la force (Unity
gives strength). The red cap of liberty, removed by the
Duvalier régime, has been reinstated above the palm
tree. The rival flag, of vertical black and red bands,
had been used by some independence groups in the
early 1800s and was readopted in 1964 by the now
discredited Duvalier government. Its colors have the
same meaning as those on the blue and red flag.

# HONDURAS, Republic of

FLAG RATIO 1:2

Honduras was one of the five member states of the United Provinces of Central America and, like the other constituent states (Costa Rica, El Salvador, Guatemala and Nicaragua) has retained a blue and white tribanded flag based on the federation's flag, itself modelled on that of Argentina. Honduras' flag was adopted in 1866, with the five central stars representing a desire for the rebirth of the federation. The state flag has the five stars appearing in an arc under the national arms: a triangle, representing equality and justice stands on a shore behind two towers, denoting independence. These are contained in an oval, banded with the motto Libre, Soberana, Independiente (Free, Sovereign, Independent) and the date of independence: September 15, 1821. Above this are arrow tails, possibly representing the indigenous population, while down the sides of the oval curl two cornucopiae, to represent the land's natural bounty. Finally, a landscape below the oval depicts trees and industrial motifs, representing the nation's forests and natural resources.

# HONG KONG, Colony of

FLAG RATIO 1:2

Hong Kong was occupied by Britain in 1841, and the Blue Ensign has been flown there since that time. The coat of arms of the colony dates from 1959, and appears inside a white disc in the fly. A shield features a naval crown above and, below, two three-sailed junks. The shield's supporters are a golden lion, to represent Britain, and a golden dragon, symbolizing Hong Kong. Another British lion appears above the shield, holding a pearl. A scroll at its base bears the name of the colony. Hong Kong was leased from China by Britain for 99 years in 1898, and is due to revert to Chinese rule in 1997.

# HUNGARY, Republic of

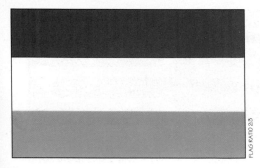

FLAG RATIO 2:3

The colors of the Hungarian flag have their origins as far back as the 9th century, when Árpad, leader of the Magyars (rulers of Hungary until the 13th century), adopted a plain red flag as his own. After the country's conversion in the 10th century, a cross on a white field was used instead, and by the 15th century, the combination of red, white and green was accepted as the national colors. Their horizontal tricolor pattern was adopted in 1848, the year of revolutions in Europe, and was modelled, not surprisingly, on the French tricolor, being used as the rallying banner for those who wanted independence from the Hapsburg Empire. After the fall of Communism in Hungary in 1989–90, the original national arms were restored and, used with the plain tricolor, they form the state flag. They include a representation of the arms of Árpad and the traditional crown of St. Stephen, first Christian king of Hungary in the 10th century.

# ICELAND, Republic of

FLAG RATIO 18:25

Invaded and colonized by Vikings from Norway in
the 9th century, Iceland has the distinction of having
held the first parliament in Europe, in 930. The republic was ruled by the King of Norway in the 13th and
14th centuries. It passed to Denmark at the same time
as Norway lost its independence to the Danes. The
current flag was adopted in 1918 when Iceland
became a separate realm in the Kingdom of Denmark,
and became the national flag on independence in
1944. The flag is the same as the Norwegian flag –
itself modelled on the Danish – with the positions of
the blue and red colors reversed. The adoption of a
Scandinavian cross and Norwegian colors shows quite
clearly that Icelandic affiliations still lie with the
Norse countries.

# INDIA, Republic of

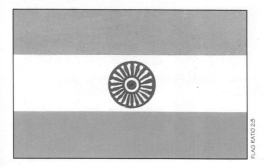

FLAG RATIO 2:3

The flag of the Indian National Congress, established
in 1885 to channel the forces for independence from
Britain, was the one which ultimately came to be used
as the basis for the national flag in 1947. The layout
was influenced by the French tricolor, and the colors
are symbolic: saffron to represent courage and
sacrifice; white to represent truth and peace; and
green to represent faith and chivalry. The Congress
flag's central motif of a spinning wheel suggested by
Gandhi, was replaced by the symbolic motif of a blue
*charkha*, or Buddhist wheel. The *charkha* comes from
the Indian national arms, depicting four lions, one
facing each direction, standing on a pedestal into
which four wheels are set. The arms are taken from
the capital, or upper part, of a column erected by the
first Buddhist emperor, Asoka, in the holy city of
Sarnath in the 3rd century BC.

# INDONESIA, Republic of

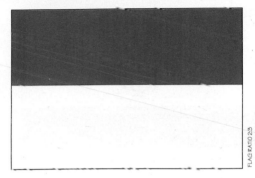

FLAG RATIO 2:3

The Majapahit Empire in 13th-century Indonesia had
a red and white flag as its banner, and these colors –
considered to be holy colors in Indonesia at that time
- were used in the region throughout medieval and
early modern times. They were revived in the 20th
century as an expression of nationalism against the
Dutch who had controlled Indonesia through the
Dutch East India Company since the 18th century.
The current flag was first used this century in the
1920s, being adopted officially as the national flag of
the republic in 1945 when the country declared its
independence. Its red over white bands stand for
courage, and justice and purity respectively. Except
for its proportions, it is identical to the flag of
Monaco.

# IRAN, Islamic Republic of

FLAG RATIO 1:3

The colors of the Iranian flag are traditional, probably
dating from at least the 18th century and they can be
interpreted as representing the Islamic religion
(green), peace (white) and courage (red). They were
designed in tricolor form in 1907. The flag's
centerpiece formerly comprised a lion with a sword
standing before a rising sun, with a crown above, but
all traditional flags and banners were abolished after
the abdication of the Shah in 1979. The new
centerpiece is a composite of various elements representing different facets of Islam which, when combined in this device, represent Allah (God). The
markings in white along the edges of the red and
green bands repeat the inscription Allah-o-Akbar
(God is Great) 22 times. The number is representative
of the date in the Muslim calendar when Ayatollah
Khomeini, founder of the Islamic Republic, returned
home to Iran.

# IRAQ, Republic of

FLAG RATIO 2:3

The Pan-Arab colors of black, green, white and red were adopted by the nationalist movements of many Arab nations in the early 20th century as they fought to free themselves from the control of the Turkish Ottoman Empire. The common colors fostered the idea of a federation between them, and traditionally they are said to represent the qualities of adherents of Islam: courage (red), generosity (white), the triumphs of Islam (black) and the religion itself (green). The present pattern of Iraq's flag dates from 1963, when the royal régime established after the First World War, was overthrown. It was based on the Egyptian flag of that period, with the same patterning of bands. The three stars in the center band represent the then-hoped-for unity of Iraq, Syria and Egypt, which never materialized. The flag's most recent addition, the Islamic slogan Allah-o-Akbar (God is Great) was adopted in 1991 during the Gulf War.

111

# IRELAND, *Republic of*

FLAG RATIO 1:2

The tricolor of Ireland was based on that of France
and was first used by the nationalists of the Young
Ireland movement in 1848, a year of revolution
throughout Europe, in their struggle for freedom
from Britain. Its colors represent the Catholic, Gaelic
and Anglo-Norman communities (green), and the
planter group of northern Protestants (orange). The
white in the center signifies a hope of peace and trust
between the two. It was adopted as the flag of the
Irish Free State in 1920, in preference to the Green
Flag – comprising a gold harp, supposedly of Irish
king Brian Boru, on an emerald green field – which
had been favored by the Home Rule movement. The
Green Flag today is used as the jack of the Irish Navy,
while the flag of the President features the same motif
on a blue field.

# ISRAEL, State of

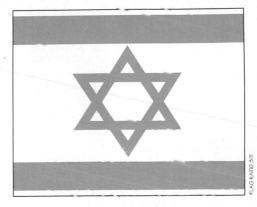

FLAG RATIO 8:11

The instantly recognizable flag of Israel bears in its center the Magen David, or Star of David, a Jewish emblem for over 700 years. The pattern of white and blue bands derives from the pattern on the *tallit*, the Jewish prayer shawl. The design emerged in the late 19th century and had its origins in the Zionist movement, the nationalist movement which sought to reestablish a Jewish homeland in Palestine. It was officially adopted as the national flag on the establishment of the State of Israel in 1948. The ensigns also feature the star, while the flag of the President features the official emblem of the state, the *menorah*, the seven-branched candlestick which is an ancient symbol of the Jewish people.

# ITALY, Italian Republic

FLAG RATIO 2:3

Based on the flag of the French Republic, the Italian tricolor was first used in 1796 in northern Italy after the peaceful French annexation of areas there, releasing it from centuries of Spanish and Austrian Hapsburg domination. The tricolor became a popular nationalist banner in the wars of independence which continued throughout the 19th century. Successful campaigns were fought by Garibaldi's Volunteer Troops to expel foreign powers from Italy, and minor states united through plebiscite. The Kingdom of Italy was finally proclaimed in 1861 under King Victor Emmanuel II of Savoy, and Rome became the capital after its annexation in 1870. The green, white and red tricolor became the national flag, bearing the arms of Savoy in the center. These were removed in 1946 when Italy became a republic. The provinces of Italy each have their own flags.

# IVORY COAST,
## Republic of Côte d'Ivoire

FLAG RATIO 2:3

A colony of France from the late 19th century until it gained its independence in 1960, the Ivory Coast is another country which has based its flag on that of the French tricolor. The colors are said to represent progress and the northern plains, or savannah (orange), hope and the agriculture of the south (green) and national unity (white). Coincidentally and significantly, green and white are also the colors of the Parti Démocratique de la Côte d'Ivoire (Ivory Coast Democratic Party), which led the country to independence and has subsequently banned all rival political opposition. The Ivory Coast flag is similar to that of Ireland, with the colors reversed and with different proportions.

# JAMAICA

FLAG RATIO 1:2

A saltire forms the main feature of the flag of Jamaica, but it is used purely as a design feature and does not represent any martyr or saint. The gold saltire divides the flag into four triangles: two green, at the top and bottom, and two black, at the hoist and fly. The colors used represent the island's natural resources, and the sun (gold), its agricultural wealth and hope (green) and the hardships which have been overcome and to be faced (black). Together, the colors symbolize the motto, "Hardships there are but the land is green and the sun shineth." The flag was officially adopted in 1962 when Jamaica became independent from Britain.

# JAPAN

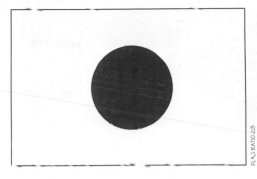

FLAG RATIO 2:3

Japan's distinctive flag is a visualization of the country's name, the "Land of the Rising Sun." According to legend, the sun was the ancestor of the imperial dynasty, and it is one of the oldest heraldic devices, having been used by the Japanese emperors for at least 600, and possibly for more than 1000 years. The national flag is the Hi-no-maru, or Sun Disc, and features a red sun on a plain white field. Despite its long traditions, it was first used as the national flag as recently as 1860 during a visit to the United States of America by the first diplomatic delegation sent abroad from Japan. The Japanese naval ensign also features the sun disc on a white field, but set slightly towards the fly and radiating 16 red rays.

# JORDAN, Hashemite Kingdom of

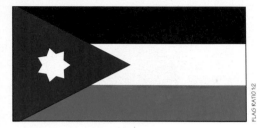

FLAG RATIO 1:2

As a part of the Turkish Ottoman Empire at the beginning of the 20th century, Jordan was one of several aspirant nations which adopted the Pan-Arab colors of black, red, white and green, all expressive of Arab nationalism; the green color has additional symbolizm, in that it is traditionally associated with Islam and its followers. In 1921 the green and white bands were transposed from their positions on the flag which had been used by the independence movement in the 1918 revolt against the Turks. In 1928 the official version of the flag saw the addition of a seven-pointed white star to the red triangle in the hoist. This has been interpreted as representing the first seven verses of the Koran, the basis of the Islamic religion, and the star is what distinguishes the Jordanian flag from that used by the Palestinian Arabs.

# KAZAKHSTAN, Republic of

The new flag of Kazakhstan was adopted in June 1992, the year after the break-up of the Union of Soviet Socialist Republics, of which Kazakhstan had been a member. On the sky-blue field is a golden sun and a soaring eagle, and in the hoist is a vertical stripe described as the "national ornamentation." The blue field represents the sky, and the sun and the eagle stand for the lofty aspirations of the Kazakh people. The blue is of a similar color to that used in the country's old SSR flag. The eagle itself is of a species known locally as the *berkut*, or steppe eagle.

# KENYA, Republic of

FLAG RATIO 5:9

Kenya was a British colony until it achieved independence in 1963, and its flag was adopted in that year also. It consists of three horizontal bands of black, red and green, separated by two narrow bands of white. The three bands are said to represent the African people, the blood common to all humanity, and the fertility of the land of Kenya, respectively. The central emblem of a Masai shield and crossed spears represents the defense of national freedom (the Masai were a noted warrior people). The colors are also those of Jomo Kenyatta's Kenya African National Union Party, leaders of the independence movement and the party which formed the government until 1992. The white bands on the flag stand for peace and national unity, the color being from the flag of the rival Kenya African Democratic Union Party.

# KIRGHIZIA

FLAG RATIO 1:2

In 1992, the year after the break-up of the USSR, the new flag of this former Soviet Socialist Republic came into being. It comprises a 40-rayed sun centered in a field of red. The sun's rays stand for the 40 tribes which merged to become the Kyrgyz nation, and the national hero, Manas the Noble, is represented by the red field. Within the sun is depicted a bird's-eye view of a yurt, the traditional tent used by the nomadic people of the steppes. The roof, or *tunduk*, of the yurt, represents the traditional heart and home of these nomadic tribes.

# KIRIBATI, Republic of

Formerly known as the Gilbert Islands, Kiribati, together with the Ellice Islands (now Tuvalu) was a British protectorate from 1892 and a colony from 1916. The process of separation of the two island groups began in 1975, and Kiribati (the local pronunciation of the word "Gilberts") achieved independence in 1979. The flag was adopted in the same year and has blue and white wavy bands, representing the Pacific Ocean, over which a sun is rising in a red sky. A local yellow frigate bird flies over the scene. The flag was based on the arms of the former colony.

# KOREA (North), Democratic People's Republic of

FLAG RATIO 1:2

Korea was a united kingdom for over five centuries until the Japanese invasion and annexation of 1910. Its liberation after the Second World War meant subsequent occupations, this time by Soviet forces in the north and American ones in the south. Soviet troops withdrew in 1948 but the government of North Korea remained Communist, a fact reflected in its flag. The flag also was adopted in 1948 and uses the blue, red and white of the traditional Korean standard, laid out in a new pattern. Three horizontal bands of blue, red and blue are separated by two narrower bands of white. In the red band, set towards the hoist and in a white roundel, is the red, five-pointed star of Communism. There have been moves towards reunification of the two parts of Korea in recent years.

# KOREA (South), Republic of

FLAG RATIO 2:3

This flag is based on one which had been used as the flag of the united kingdom of Korea in the second half of the 19th century. It has been in use in its present form since 1950, after the partition of the old kingdom into its northern and southern components (see Korea, Democratic People's Republic of). The white field represents the people's purity and their desire for peace, while its central emblem is the red and blue yin-yang symbol, depicting the concepts of creation and development through duality and balance. Surrounding this are four black trigrams, or *kwae* symbols, which are taken from the *I Ching* (the ancient Chinese book of divination and philosophy) and represent the four seasons, the four compass points, the four elements and the sun, the moon, the earth and heaven. They denote the process of yin and yang going through a spiral of change and growth.

# KUWAIT, State of

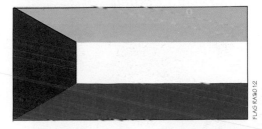

FLAG RATIO 1:2

The Pan-Arab colors, representing the desired unity
of the Arab nations, comprise the colors of the flag of
Kuwait. Previously a part of the Turkish Ottoman
Empire, Kuwait had been a British protectorate from
1899, becoming independent in 1961. The flag was
adopted in the same year, and consists of a horizontal
tricolor of green, white and red, with a black
trapezium in the hoist. The idea for this slightly
unusual shape may have come from a similar one in
the flag of Iraq until the late 1950s. The colors are also
symbolic in their own right: according to a well-
known Arabic poem, green is the color of fertility,
white signifies glorious deeds, red stands for chivalry
and warriorship, and black symbolizes bravery in
war. The Kuwaiti flag was abolished by the Iraqis who
invaded and occupied the country in 1990, asserting
traditional claims to Kuwait, but it was re-established
after the successful campaign by a multi-national
military force to expel the Iraquis in 1991.

# LAOS, Lao People's Democratic Republic

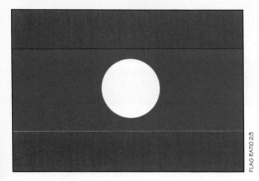

FLAG RATIO 2:3

This is one of the few Communist flags which does not use the five-pointed star as an emblem. Adopted when the country became a republic in 1975, the flag has a white disc in its center, symbolizing the unity of the people under the leadership of the Lao People's Revolutionary Party. The red color stands for the blood shed by the people in defence of their country, and the blue symbolizes the nation's wealth. The flag was that of the Pathet Lao, or Lao Patriotic Front, who battled with the royalist government forces for control of the country after the winning of independence from France. This flag replaced the royalist flag of three elephants standing beneath a parasol, on five steps, representing in its disparate elements the monarchy, the people and their Buddhist faith.

# LATVIA, Republic of

FLAG RATIO 1:2

There are conflicting stories of the origin of the maroon and white triband of Latvia. It was first mentioned in a Latvian chronicle of a battle in 1280, where a battalion from Cesis, a northern region, bore a red flag with a white stripe which was also the banner of a castle there. Another legend refers to a leader of a Latvian tribe who was wounded in battle and wrapped in a white sheet. The part of the sheet on which he was lying remained white, but the two edges which were folded over him were stained by his blood. Latvia was invaded sporadically over the centuries by the Swedes and Poles, finally falling under Russian control from 1789–1918. Towards the end of this period, use of the flag by nationalist groups increased but was forbidden by the Tsarist forces. The flag finally was adopted officially in 1923, although Latvia lost its independence to the Soviet Union from 1940 to 1991. Since the ending of Soviet rule the national flag has been in use once more.

# LEBANON, Republic of

FLAG RATIO 2:3

The symbol of a cedar tree, an ancient symbol of Lebanon since biblical times, is the centerpiece of the flag of the Lebanese Republic. Following the First World War and the break up of the Ottoman Empire, Lebanon was administered by France, and the cedar appeared on the white band of the French tricolor. The present flag was adopted on independence in 1943. The red and white bands are thought to have been the colors of the Lebanese Legion in the First World War, and officially they represent respectively the sacrifices of the people for independence, and purity, while the cedar tree symbolizes happiness and prosperity for the country.

# LESOTHO, Kingdom of

FLAG RATIO 2:3

The flag of Lesotho has changed in recent years, with
the one originally adopted on independence in 1966
having been dropped. The national flag then had a
blue field, with narrow green and red vertical bands
at the hoist. A white straw hat, traditional symbol of
the Basotho people of the country, appeared in the
center of the blue field. However, the flag's colors
were those of the leading Lesotho National Party, and
a new flag was deemed necessary after a coup in
1986. The present flag is divided diagonally from the
top of the fly to the base of the hoist. The upper half
is white and bears a shield with two crossed weapons
at the hoist, representing the Basotho peoples' means
of maintaining peace and independence, while the
white itself represents peace. The broad blue band in
the lower half represents rain, while the green
triangle symbolizes prosperity.

# LIBERIA, Republic of

FLAG RATIO 10:19

Liberia was settled in 1822 by the American
Colonization Society as a homeland for freed
American slaves. A similar form of flag to that
ultimately adopted, was in use at that time but was
modified to its present form on independence in 1847.
Its design is clearly based on the American Stars and
Stripes. There are 11 red and white stripes in the field,
to represent the 11 men who signed Liberia's declaration of independence. The blue of the canton stands
for Africa, while the five-pointed white star refers to
Liberia's status at the time of its gaining independence
as the only independent African nation.

# LIBYA, Great Socialist People's Libyan Arab Jamahiriya

FLAG RATIO 2:5

Prior to 1977, the Libyan national flag comprised the Pan-Arab colors of red, white and black in a design identical to that of Egypt, with whom Libya was in federation at that time. However, in 1977 Egypt made a peace treaty with its traditional enemy, Israel, in a move that angered many Arab nations. In a reaction to this Israeli–Egyptian pact, Libya adopted its current flag, the plain green field symbolizing its Green Revolution (which emphasized agriculture and the need for self-sufficiency in food) and the nation's continuing adherence to Islam. Two years later in 1979 Libya also left the Federation of Arab Republics, of which it had been a co-founder with Egypt and Syria.

# LIECHTENSTEIN, Principality of

FLAG RATIO 2:3

The principality of Liechtenstein was created in 1719 following the union of the countships of Vaduz and Schellenberg. The blue and red of the flag have been used as the national colors since the early 19th century, and the gold crown was added to the canton in 1937 to avoid any confusion with the flag of Haiti. When this flag is flown vertically, the crown appears rotated through 90° so that its cross continues to point towards the top of the flag. The state flag is also a bicolor of blue over red, but with the arms of Liechtenstein in the center, and without the crown in the canton.

# LITHUANIA, Republic of

FLAG RATIO 1:2

Lithuania's yellow, green and red tricolor was first adopted as the national flag in 1918, with official sanction following four years later. This flag remained in use until the republic's amalgamation into the Union of Soviet Socialist Republics in 1940. The yellow band symbolizes ripening wheat and consequently agricultural wealth and freedom from want. Green recalls the country's forests, and hope, while red represents love of the country, as well as referring to the color of the old banners of the medieval kingdom of Lithuania. The tricolor began to reappear in public in early 1990, prior to the disintegration of the USSR.

# LUXEMBOURG, Grand Duchy of

The colors of the Grand Duchy's flag derive directly from its arms, which are centuries old: a shield which forms the centerpiece of the arms has a blue-and-white-striped background, with a red, crowned, two-tailed lion rampant in the center, and these colors were adopted for the flag. Its design dates from the mid 19th century and was probably influenced by the French tricolor, but the flag itself was not officially adopted until 1972. It is similar in appearance to the flag of the Netherlands, but the Luxembourg blue is of a paler shade and the flags' proportions are slightly different.

# MACEDONIA, Republic of

FLAG RATIO 1:2

The Yugoslavian province of Macedonia declared itself independent in April 1992, but immediately found itself in disagreement with its neighbor, Greece, over the adoption of its emblem, known as the Macedonian Star. The star came to prominence in recent times when it was used as an emblem among Macedonians living in Australia, and it was adopted for the new flag in preference to the traditional Macedonian colors of black and red. The star was said to be derived originally from a decoration on the gold coffin of the Greek king Philip II of Macedon, father of Alexander the Great, and is used, in a slightly different form, as the emblem of the Greek province of Macedonia. International recognition of the new country has been opposed by Greece, which fears territorial claims on its own province of Macedonia, and it was allowed to enter the United Nations only on the unique condition that its flag would not be displayed there.

# MADAGASCAR, Democratic Republic of

FLAG RATIO 2:3

Madagascar, a large island in the western Indian Ocean off the southeast coast of Africa, has been a traditional destination for immigrants from Southeast Asia, and this demographic trend is reflected in the colors of its flag. The red and white are said to represent the island's first inhabitants: the Hova people from Southeast Asia (red and white are the colors traditionally associated with the region; see, for example, the flag of Indonesia), as well as the Africans of the island. The green is said to represent the people of the coastal region; this color was added when the flag was adopted in 1958, two years before full independence from France was gained.

# MALAWI, Republic of

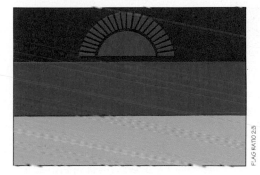

FLAG RATIO 2:3

The ruling Malawi Congress Party used its flag, a
horizontal tricolor of black, red and green, as the
basis for the design of the new national flag when the
country became independent in 1964. Its colors are
symbolic: black, to represent the African people; red,
for the blood of the freedom fighters; and green, to
symbolize the land and its fertility. The rising sun was
added to the black band in 1964 to symbolize a new
dawn for Malawi and for Africa, and is based on the
sun which appears, also against a black background,
on the Malawi coat of arms.

# MALAYSIA, Federation of

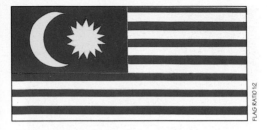

FLAG RATIO 1:2

At first sight the Malaysian national flag is
reminiscent of the American Stars and Stripes, and it
is probable that this was the inspiration for its design,
although the similarity of colors is probably
coincidental. The red and white of the stripes are colors which are traditionally used in Southeast Asia,
while the blue of the canton stands for the unity of
the peoples of Malaysia. The yellow of the star and
crescent is the royal color of the rulers of Malaysia,
while the symbols themselves represent the
dominant religion, Islam. The Malaysian federation's
original 14 member states are represented in the 14
stripes, and in the 14 points of the star in the canton.
Although Singapore left the federation in 1965, two
years after it was founded, the flag remained
unchanged, and the extra stripe and point are now
said to represent the federal government.

# MALDIVES, Republic

FLAG RATIO 2:3

The Maldives are a coral atoll in the Indian Ocean comprising over 1,000 islands; the local name for the group is The Thousand Islands. As with the flags of other states in the region, the color red features prominently; in fact, the original flag of the islands had only a plain red field. The islands, which had been a British protectorate since 1887, became independent in 1965, and the present design was adopted in the same year. The colors represent the sacrifice of the heroes of the independence struggle (red), and progress and prosperity (green). The central panel contains a white crescent, recognized as a symbol of the Islamic religion.

# MALI, Republic of

FLAG RATIO 2:3

Mali was formerly occupied by France, becoming a colony at the start of the 20th century. Before it became independent, it formed the Mali Federation, with Senegal, but that country left the federation when Mali gained its independence in 1960. The influence of the French tricolor can be seen in the proportions and design of the flag. Green, yellow and red are the colors of the Pan-African movement, used by so many former colonial states who gained their independence at that time, and are expressive of a wish for African unity. The same basic flag has been used since 1959, although previously with a black human stick-figure in the center of the yellow band. This was dropped in 1961 to leave the present plain tricolor.

# MALTA, Republic of

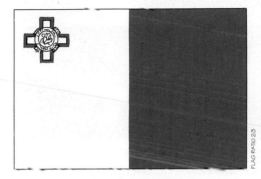

FLAG RATIO 2:3

According to tradition the national colors of white and red were given to the Maltese in 1090 by Count Roger the Norman, who had landed on the island to expel the Arabs. In recognition of the hospitality he received, Roger gave the Maltese part of the pennant of the Hautevilles to serve as their colors. The red-fimbriated George Cross which appears in the canton was added in 1943 after the award of that medal to the people of the island for their heroism and resilience in withstanding the Axis powers' siege of 1940–43. A previous blue canton disappeared from behind the St. George's cross when the island gained its independence from Britain after a century and a half of colonial rule. The traditional four-armed, eight-pointed Maltese Cross appears in white on a red field to form the civil ensign.

# MARSHALL ISLANDS,
## Republic of the

FLAG RATIO 1:2

Formerly a part of the United States Trust Territory of the Pacific Islands, the Marshall Islands split from Micronesia in order to become independent and self-governing. The new government took office in 1979 and the country acquired a new flag at the same time. As with so many island states in the Pacific, blue and white are the principal colors and a star motif features prominently. The star represents the Marshall Islands themselves, and its 24 points each of the islands' districts. The four elongated compass points of the star express the islanders' Christian faith, while the star's position, in a field of blue and above the two bands, suggest the islands' location, in the Pacific Ocean and slightly north of the equator. The white and orange stripes represent hope and wealth for the new country.

# MAURITANIA, Islamic Republic of

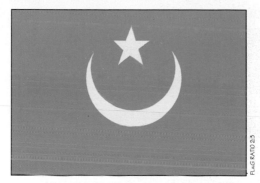

FLAG RATIO 2:3

As with the other former French colonies of North
Africa, Mauritania chose not to use the tricolor as the
basis of its flag and instead elected to depict the
predominance of the Muslim religion in the country.
The crescent and five-pointed star are traditional
Islamic motifs, as is the color green which appears in
the field. They also reflect the country's appellation
of an Islamic republic. The flag was adopted in 1959,
the year before Mauritania won its independence
from France.

# MAURITIUS

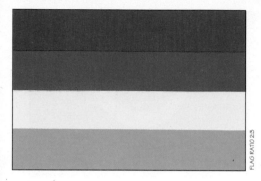

The colors of the flag of Mauritius are those which appear on its coat of arms, which dates from 1906. The flag itself was adopted in 1968, on independence from Britain, by whom the island had been ruled since 1815. The colors are said to have a particular significance: red represents the country's independence; blue is the color of the Indian Ocean; yellow symbolizes the country's bright future; and green stands for its lush vegetation. Although red, yellow and green are also the colors of the Pan-African movement, the adoption of those colors for use in national flags has largely been a Central and Western African practice, so it is unlikely that they carry the same significance here.

# MEXICO, United Mexican States

FLAG RATIO 4:7

The flag of Mexico was modelled on the design of the French tricolor, a ubiquitous symbol of liberty, at a time when Mexico was trying to achieve its independence from Spain. The colors were those of the independence movement, and are also said to represent the three guarantees given by the freedom fighters: freedom of religious worship; independence from Spain; and the unity of the states of Mexico. The tricolor was adopted as the national flag when Mexico became independent in 1821. The central emblem is the national arms, added in their present form in 1968. They depict an eagle perched on a cactus holding a snake in its beak, and reflect an Aztec legend of the founding of Mexico City, in which the place to be built upon would be signified by an eagle standing on a cactus.

# MICRONESIA,
## Federated States of

FLAG RATIO 10:19

When the Marshall Islands and Palau broke away from the original United States Trust Territory of Micronesia in 1979, the country was renamed the Federated States of Micronesia and a new flag was adopted. The old one had been based on the field of blue of the United Nations flag, as the islands had been entrusted to the United States of America by the UN; six stars represented the original six areas of the islands. The four stars of the current flag represent the members left in the federation: Kosrae, Pohnpei, Truk and Yap. Each of the separate states also has its own flag.

# MOLDOVA, Republic of

FLAG RATIC 1:2

The flag of the new Republic of Moldova was adopted
in late 1990, shortly before the official break-up of the
old Union of Soviet Socialist Republics. It bears a
resemblance to the flag of Romania, and the central
arms, featuring a spread eagle, are not unlike those
previously used by the Romanians. Here, the bull's
head symbolizes Moldova, while the colors represent
the past, present and future of the country as well as
its democratic principles and historical traditions, and
the equality of all its citizens.

# MONACO, Principality of

FLAG RATIO 4:5

The Grimaldi family became rulers of Monaco in the 13th century, and are still in power today. The state's relations with France and Italy have always been close, but Monaco has retained its independence, and a constitution was established in 1911. The colors of the flag are taken from the ruling family's coat of arms, which are of medieval origin: the central shield of the arms is covered by red and white lozenges, or diamonds. The flag was adopted in 1881 and is distinguished from the similar red over white bicolor of Indonesia by its squarer proportions.

# MONGOLIA, Republic of

FLAG RATIO1:2

The flag of Mongolia was adopted in 1940, and its colors and elements represent both nationalism and Buddhism. The two red bands at fly and hoist were originally intended to represent the victory of Communism in the 1920s, but they are now said to symbolize progress and prosperity. The central blue band is recognized as representing the Mongol peoples and their patriotism. The Golden Soyonbo which appears at the hoist is a Buddhist symbol whose shapes symbolize aspects of the Buddhist faith: for example, eternal life, represented by the sun and moon; and the balance of life and nature, represented by the yin-yang symbol. It also represents the independence, sovereignty and spirit of Mongolia. The flag itself was adopted in 1940 and was confirmed officially in 1949.

# MOROCCO, Kingdom of

FLAG RATIO 2:3

Red has been the traditional color of the flag of Morocco since the 16th century, and is said to represent the blood ties between the royal family and the prophet Mohammed. The green pentacle, depicting the Seal of Solomon, was added to the center in 1915, and the flag has remained in its present form since then. Like other French-occupied areas and colonies in northern Africa, but unlike those to the south, Morocco has not taken any adaptation of the tricolor to use as its flag. Even during French occupation, the only evidence was a tricolor in the canton of the civil ensign.

# MOZAMBIQUE, Republic of

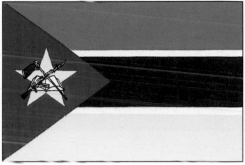

FLAG RATIO 5:8

Mozambique's flag is based on that of its leading political party, the Frente de Libertação de Moçambique (FRELIMO), who led the country to independence from Portuguese rule in 1975. The colors are symbolic: green for the land and its riches, black for the African continent, and gold for the mineral wealth, with the red triangle at the hoist symbolizing the struggle for independence, and two narrow white fimbriations to represent peace. The emblem in the triangle shows an open book under a crossed rifle and hoe, representing teachers and education, the army and the fight for freedom, and agricultural work and its importance to the economy, respectively. These are backed by the five-pointed gold star of Communism and Internationalism. This flag was adopted in 1983 and is a modified version of that which was used since independence.

# MYANMAR, Union of

FLAG RATIO 5:9

The modern flag of Myanmar (or Burma, as it was previously called) has its origins during the Second World War, when the resistance movement, fighting the occupying Japanese forces, adopted a flag with a plain red field with a white star in the canton. This was modified in 1948, when the country became independent of the British Empire, to a red field with a blue canton, with five smaller stars surrounding one large one, representative of the country's diverse ethnic components and their unity in one nation. The design was changed again in 1974, with the coming to power of a Communist régime: the five stars became 14, to represent the 14 states of the country, and they form a circle around a gear wheel and two ears of paddy, showing the union of industry and agriculture. Today, the red stands for the courage of the people, the blue for peace and integrity, and the white for purity and virtue. The country's name was changed in 1989, and a democratic government elected in 1990.

# NAMIBIA, Republic of

FLAG RATIO 2:3

Formerly the trust territory of South West Africa, Namibia had been occupied by South Africa since early in this century and, despite repeated United Nations calls for its independence, remained so until 1990. The national flag adopted on independence was based on the winning entry in a competition and, coincidentally, uses the colors found in the flags of certain Namibian political parties. Blue symbolizes the sky, the Atlantic Ocean and the importance of water and rain; red represents the Namibian people and their aspiration of a fair and equitable society; while green stands for vegetation and agricultural resources. The white fimbriations symbolize peace and unity, while the sun depicts life and energy, and its gold color the sun's warmth, the golden plains, and color of the desert.

# NAURU, Republic of

FLAG RATIO 1:2

In common with the flags of some other Pacific island nations, the flag of Nauru depicts the nation's geographical location. Represented by the star, Nauru appears set in the Pacific Ocean just to the south of the Equator. The 12 points of the star are said to represent the 12 indigenous tribes of the island. The flag was adopted on independence from the joint administration of Australia, New Zealand and Britain in 1968, and was the winning entry in a competition.

# NEPAL, Kingdom of

FLAG RATIO 4:3 ALONG STRAIGHT EDGES

The flag of Nepal is the only national flag which is
not rectangular, being based upon two separate pennants, flown one above the other, which belonged to
rival branches of the Rana dynasty, the former rulers
of Nepal. The two pennants were first joined in the
last century, but the flag was not adopted officially
until 1962, after the establishment of a constitutional
form of government. The white sun and horizontal
crescent moon are now said to express the hope that
Nepal itself will last as long as the sun and moon.
These motifs appear in white against a red background
(crimson being the national color), and a blue border
edges the whole flag.

# NETHERLANDS, Kingdom of the

FLAG RATIO 2:3

Possibly the first revolutionary tricolor, the Dutch
flag of red, white and blue may have been used as a
model for the French tricolor, itself a seminal
influence on flags throughout the world. The flag was
first used in the late 16th century in the struggle for
independence from the Spanish Hapsburg Empire, of
which the Netherlands was then a part. The colors,
originally orange, white and blue, were changed to
red, white and blue in the mid 17th century and were
probably taken from the livery and arms of William
of Orange, the main leader of the independence
movement: a blue hunting horn with silver
mountings, hanging on a red cord. All the provinces
of the Netherlands have their own flags.

# NETHERLANDS ANTILLES

FLAG RATIO 2:3

A self-governing territory of the Netherlands, the Antilles are two island groups in the Caribbean which became part of the Dutch Empire in the 17th century. They became autonomous in 1954, and the flag was adopted originally in 1959. The red and blue bands of the Netherlands have been used, in a cross pattern on a white field, while the five stars represent the islands themselves: Bonaire, Curaçao, Saba, St. Eustatius and St. Maarten. There were formerly six stars, the sixth representing Aruba, but that island became self-governing in 1986. Aruba's flag has a blue field with white-fimbriated, four-pointed red star in the canton and two yellow stripes near the foot, symbolizing Aruba's independence yet closeness to its Caribbean neighbors. The other islands, except St. Eustatius, now have their own flags.

# NEW ZEALAND

FLAG RATIO 1:2

New Zealand's recent history as a colony of Britain is reflected in the appearance of its flag, which is based on the British Blue Ensign, with the country's distinguishing badge set in the fly: a group of four white-fimbriated, red five-pointed stars, a stylized representation of the Southern Cross constellation and a design feature commonly found on the flags of many countries in the southern hemisphere. This flag had originally been designed in 1869 for use at sea, and was officially adopted as the national flag on land in 1902, around the time that Australia was adopting a similar flag.

# NICARAGUA, Republic of

FLAG RATIO 3:5

Nicaragua was one of the five member states of the United Provinces of Central America from 1823–38, along with Costa Rica, El Salvador, Guatemala and Honduras. The flags of all five states are based on the old blue, white and blue triband of the federation, itself based originally on the flag of Argentina. The El Salvadorean and Nicaraguan flags of today differ only in the shades of blue used. The state flag bears the arms in the center of the white band, and these, too, are very similar to the federation arms: five peaks rise up between two stretches of water, representing the five federation members, and the Atlantic and Pacific. The radiating red cap of liberty symbolizes the dawn of a new era, while the rainbow over the whole scene signifies hope. The image appears within an equilateral triangle, a traditional symbol of liberty, with the country's name and a reference to the United Provinces, in the words America Central, around all.

# NIGER, Republic of

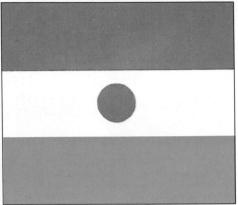

FLAG RATIO 6:7

Niger, like other former French colonies, used the tricolor as a design model for its own flag on independence. It was part of French West Africa from the beginning of this century until 1960, and the present flag was adopted in 1959 in anticipation of independence the following year. The colors symbolize the country's physical features: orange represents the Sahara Desert which occupies much of the north of the country, green the grasslands of the south, and white the River Niger flowing between the two. The orange disc in the center symbolizes the sun. The Ivory Coast, also once a part of French West Africa, is the only other African country using these colors.

# NIGERIA, Federal Republic of

FLAG RATIO 1:2

Nigeria was a British colony from the 19th century until 1960, when the flag of the new nation was adopted. The present flag was the winning entry in a competition held in 1959. The green, white and green vertical triband depicts the country. the River Niger, symbolized in the white band, runs through forests on either side, represented by the green bands. The colors have further significance: green also represents agriculture, Nigeria's main source of wealth, and the white band is said to symbolize unity and peace.

# NIUE

FLAG RATIO 1:2

The flag of Niue is based on that of New Zealand, of whom the island has been an autonomous dependency since 1974. The flag itself was adopted in 1975. The yellow field represents the warmth of mutual friendship between Niue and New Zealand. The four five-pointed stars of the Southern Cross constellation, on the fly of the New Zealand flag, appear in yellow on the arms of the cross of St. George in the Union Jack in the canton, and the central yellow star, set within a blue disc, represents Niue itself. Many Pacific Ocean nations choose to represent themselves in their flags by the use of stars.

# NORTHERN MARIANAS

FLAG RATIO 10:19

The field of blue and prominent white star mark out
this flag as belonging to a Pacific state, as these characteristics are shared by several countries in the region.
The blue is derived from the blue on the United
Nations flag, as Northern Marianas was formerly a
trust territory of the UN, administered by the United
States of America after years of Japanese occupation.
Northern Marianas broke away from the rest of the
sprawling US Pacific Trust Territory in 1976, and its flag
was adopted that year. The white star, representing the
islands, appears in front of a chalice-shaped stone symbol, a Polynesian *taga*, which was used as a symbol of
authority. Here it represents the ancient culture and
traditions of the people and is surrounded by a flower
garland.

# NORWAY, Kingdom of

FLAG RATIO 8:11

Norway's flag displays in the off-center Scandinavian cross its affiliation with the Norse countries. Norway was subject to Denmark from 1397 to 1814, after which it passed to Sweden. The two countries' union was not a happy one, and there was agitation for independence within Norway throughout the 19th century, although the union was not dissolved officially until 1905. General use of the flag was not allowed by Sweden until the end of the 19th century. The addition of the blue cross over the white Danish one was a reference to the red, white and blue of the United States of America and the United Kingdom, as countries which were not ruled by an absolute monarch. They also referred to the colors of France, by then recognized as revolutionary colors. As in Finland and Sweden, the modern naval ensign is swallowtailed with a tongue.

# OMAN, Sultanate of

FLAG RATIO 2:3

The accession of Sultan Quabus bin Sa'id in 1970 saw the adoption of a new Omani flag. Until then, the country (called Muscat and Oman) had used the centuries-old red banner of the indigenous peoples, the Kharijte Muslims. Red has been retained in the new flag, now with the addition of white and green panels in the upper and lower parts of the fly. In the canton appear the state arms in red and white: two crossed sabres feature behind a *gambia*, a traditional local dagger, and an elaborate horse bit appears in the foreground over all.

# PAKISTAN, Islamic Republic of

FLAG RATIO 2:3

The flag of Pakistan, officially adopted in 1947, is based on the flag of the All-India Muslim League, a body which spearheaded the struggle of the Muslims of South Asia for the establishment of a separate Muslim state. Pakistan gained its independence in 1947 when India was partitioned into two separate dominions on British withdrawal, and it became an Islamic Republic in 1956. The national flag is green with a white vertical bar at the hoist, a white crescent in the center and a five-pointed white star. The white and green together represent peace and prosperity, the crescent symbolizes progress, and the five-rayed star stands for light and knowledge. The green color, the star and the crescent are also, of course, traditional Islamic motifs.

# PALAU, Republic of

Originally part of the United States Trust Territory of the Pacific Islands, Palau broke away to become a self-governing republic in 1981. The flag dates from the same period. The blue field is common to the flags of many nations in this area of the world, and represents their location in the Pacific. The yellow disc, set slightly towards the hoist, represents the full moon and is a symbol of productiveness. It is also a reference to the ancient culture of the islanders and their belief that the time of the full moon is the most productive for creative tasks like planting, harvesting and fishing.

# PANAMA, *Republic of*

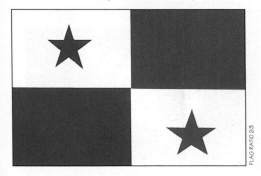

FLAG RATIO 2:3

In 1903 Panama was a province of Colombia and was closely involved in negotiations with the United States of America as a result of Colombia's refusal to allow the USA to build a canal to link the Atlantic and Pacific Oceans through its territory. Possibly as a consequence of this involvement and Panama's subsequent secession over the matter, its flag is strongly suggestive of the American Stars and Stripes, although here imbued with their own particular significance. The flag is on a quarterly design, with white and blue quarters in the hoist, and red and white in the fly. The blue and red represent contemporary Panamanian political parties – conservatives and liberals respectively – while white symbolizes a hope of peace between the two. The red star represents the supremacy of the law and the blue, public honesty and loyalty.

# PAPUA NEW GUINEA,
## Independent State of

The formation of Papua New Guinea united the former German territory of New Guinea with the Australian-administered Papua, and the country gained its independence in 1975. The distinctive national flag has two triangles of red over black. The local *kumul* bird of paradise, first used as a local motif in the late 19th century, flies across the red half, symbolizing Papua New Guinea's emergence into nationhood. The five five-pointed stars of the Southern Cross constellation appear in the black, reflecting ties with Australia and other nations of the South Pacific. Black, red and yellow are also traditional colors in Papua New Guinea. The flag was designed by a local person, and was adopted in 1971.

# PARAGUAY, Republic of

FLAG RATIO 1:2

Paraguay's flag is unusual because it bears two different badges on its obverse (shown above) and reverse sides. The red, white and blue horizontal tricolor first appeared in 1811 when Paraguay freed itself of Spanish rule. It was probably influenced by the French tricolor, itself a symbol of revolution. The present version of the flag, with new central emblems, has been in use since 1842. The obverse emblem depicts the Star of May, generally used as a symbol of freedom and independence on South American flags, and here a symbol of Paraguayan freedom from Spain (achieved on May 14, 1811). That on the reverse is the seal of the treasury, showing a lion guarding a staff on which sits a red cap of liberty, with the words Paz y Justicia (Peace and Justice), set above.

# PERU, Republic of

FLAG RATIO 2:3

The traditional explanation of the use of a red, white and red triband as the Peruvian national flag is whimsical: in 1821, General José de San Martín, who was engaged in the struggle to liberate the country from Spanish rule, saw a flock of flamingoes, with white breasts and red wings, fly over his troops. He took this to be a good omen, and declared red and white to be the colors of liberty. The veracity of this story is not known, but red and white were also colors associated with the local Inca peoples. The flag was officially adopted in 1825, after the defeat of the Spanish. The addition of the national arms to the center forms the state flag. These comprise a shield with three motifs depicting local flora, fauna and natural resources, all surrounded by a wreath.

# PHILIPPINES, Republic of the

FLAG RATIO 1:2

The Philippine flag had its origins in the liberation
movement against Spain in the 1890s. It may have been
inspired by the American flag, and was in use by the
time the islands fell to America, after the ending of the
Spanish–American war in 1898. The white triangle in
the hoist represents the liberation movement, while
the blue and red bands represent magnanimity and
courage respectively. The colors are reversed in time of
war. The large, eight-pointed yellow star in the
center of the triangle commemorates the eight
provinces who rose in revolt against Spain, while the
yellow stars at the triangle's points stand for the three
main island groups: Luzon, Mindanao and the Visayan
archipelago.

# POLAND, Republic of

FLAG RATIO 5:8

The colors of white and red which form this flag are derived from the national arms, in use since the 13th century. These depict a white eagle on a red field, and while the national flag is plain, other official flags bear the national arms. The national rising of 1830–31 against the Russians (Poland being part of the Russian Empire at this time) saw the adoption of red and white cockades by the insurgents, although the colors were proscribed after the rising was put down. The red and white flag was officially adopted in 1919, when Poland was reformed in the Versailles settlement, having been partitioned by the major powers in the previous two centuries.

# PORTUGAL

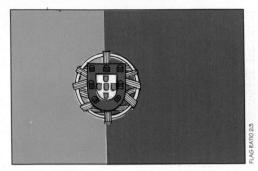

FLAG RATIO 2:3

The establishment of a republic in 1910 led to Portugal's adopting a new flag. Red and green were the republican colors, while the central emblem symbolized episodes from the imperial past. The white shield containing five blue shields represents the victory of King Alfonso Henriques over five Moorish princes at the Battle of Ourique in 1139. The five white shapes on each shield recall the five wounds of Christ, in whose name the battle was fought and to whom victory was attributed. The seven gold castles in the orle (the shield's border) stand for Portugal's expansion as a result of Alfonso's marriage in 1146. The armillary sphere behind was an early navigational instrument and represents the importance of Portuguese explorers in discovery and circumnavigation of the globe. Finally, the white shield was said to represent Portugal, the orle with the castles the Algarve, and the armillary sphere Brazil; all together, these comprised the United Kingdom of Portugal.

# PUERTO RICO, Commonwealth of

FLAG RATIO 2:3

The Puerto Rican flag looks at first glance to be identical in design to that of Cuba, but with the red and blue transposed. Indeed, both flags express a common aspiration of the islands in the 19th century – freedom from Spanish rule with the help of the United States of America. The flag of Puerto Rico came later than the Cuban one, and was based intentionally on the Cuban flag, being used by the revolutionaries during their attempts to win independence from 1895 onwards. The island fell to the USA after the Spanish–American War of 1898, and although it became self-governing in 1952 – when the flag was adopted officially – it remains a dependent territory and consequently flies its flag only alongside the Stars and Stripes.

# QATAR, State of

FLAG RATIO 11:28

The flag of Qatar is similar to that of Bahrain, with whom the country was formerly linked. The peoples of both countries are Kharijite Muslims, whose traditional banner was red. It is believed that the present maroon color came about from the action of the elements, especially the sun, on the natural red dyes formerly used for the flags. Like Bahrain, Qatar also has a nine-pointed zigzag white interlock at the hoist, deriving from a British request in the 1820s that all friendly states around the Persian Gulf add a white band to their flags. The flag evolved to its present form around the mid 19th century, and was officially adopted when Qatar became independent in 1971.

# ROMANIA

FLAG RATIO 2:3

The tricolor of Romania emerged in 1848, a year of revolution throughout Europe, as an expression of the desire for freedom from the Ottoman Empire by the provinces of Moldavia and Wallachia. The flag's original design, a horizontal tricolor, was probably, like other new flags which emerged at that time, based on the principles of liberty symbolized in the French tricolor. The bands became vertical in 1867. The colors are those of the two provinces: blue and red for Moldavia, and blue and yellow for Wallachia. From 1867 until 1990, emblems appeared in the center – first royalist, then Communist – but since the overthrow of Ceausescu, the last Communist president, the flag has been plain, making it identical to that of Chad.

# RUSSIA, Russian Federation

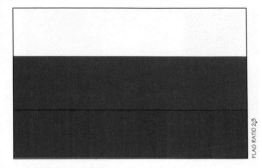

FLAG RATIO 2/3

The tricolor of Russia dates from the time of the reforming Tsar Peter the Great (1672–1725) who traveled in Europe towards the end of the 17th century, and spent some time in Amsterdam and Leiden. The colors and design of the Dutch flag were adopted and rearranged to form a white, blue and red pattern. The tricolor was not adopted officially until 1799 and fell into disuse after the Bolshevik revolution of 1917, being revived as the Russian flag in 1990 only as the Union of Soviet Socialist Republics disintegrated. The colors and design of the flag had a great influence on the Pan-Slav movement in Eastern Europe in the 19th century, with many small nations adopting them as their own.

# RWANDA, Republic of

The Pan-African colors, expressive of African
nationalism and an aspiration towards African unity,
are those which form the basis of the flag of Rwanda.
The initial letter of the state, the large "R" in the center,
distinguishes it from the flag of Guinea, with which it
is otherwise identical. Rwanda was a Belgian colony
until 1962, when an independent republic was
declared and the flag adopted officially. Its format, like
to many other revolutionary and republican flags, was
probably based on that of the French tricolor.

# ST. CHRISTOPHER AND NEVIS, Federation of

FLAG RATIO 2:3

St. Christopher (also known as St. Kitts) and Nevis, former British colonies, gained their independence in 1983, and this flag was adopted in the same year. It was the winning entry in a local competition and uses colors found in other West Indian flags. Green, yellow and red are also the colors of the Pan-African movement, although in this context the colors officially have a different significance: green represents the islands' fertility; red stands for the struggles of the people from slavery through colonialism to independence; and yellow is for the sunshine. The peoples' African heritage is acknowledged by the black, while the two white stars symbolize hope and liberty.

# ST. LUCIA, State of

The same flag design which St. Lucia used while an associated state was retained after the island's independence from Britain in 1979. The flag is a stylized depiction of St. Lucia itself: a volcanic island amid a blue sea, with three central mountains, the Pitons, in the center. The colors are symbolic in themselves: blue stands for fidelity, as well as for the Caribbean and the Atlantic surrounding the shores; gold stands for prosperity and sunshine; and black and white represent dual racial culture and harmony. The design was the winning entry in a locally held competition.

# ST. VINCENT AND THE GRENADINES

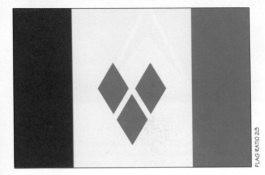

FLAG RATIO 2:3

In common with the flags of other West Indian states, that of St. Vincent emerged as the winner in a local competition. The flag in use at present is a modified version of the original. The bands of color are symbolic: blue for the sky, yellow for the sunshine, and green for the islands' lush vegetation. The "V" of diamonds in the center stands for "Vincent"; this was introduced in 1985 to replace the previous central motif of a breadfruit leaf behind the islands' arms. The original version had been adopted in 1979 when the islands became independent from Britain.

# SAN MARINO, Republic of

FLAG RATIO 3:4

Reputedly founded in the 4th century AD, San Marino is the world's smallest republic. The colors of its flag are said to represent the snowy peaked mountains and sky, and they also feature in the national arms which appear in the center of the official, state flag. A heart shaped shield, topped by a crown (a symbol of authority), contains three towers with ostrich plumes above. These depict the three towers built on Mount Titano, the main mountain in San Marino, and symbolize the republic's ability to defend itself. A laurel and oak wreath surround these, with the motto, Libertas, below, another reminder of the state's independence.

# SÃO TOMÉ AND PRÍNCIPE, Democratic Republic of

FLAG RATIO 1:2

The flag of the main liberation movement, the Movimento de Liberación de São Tomé e Príncipe (MLSP) was adopted in 1975 as the national flag of this former Portuguese colony, with a modification to the proportions of the bands. Red, green and yellow are the colors of the Pan-African movement, symbolizing African solidarity and nationalism. They were adopted by many former colonies, particularly in West Africa, on their liberation. The two black stars represent the islands themselves and their African peoples.

# SAUDI ARABIA, Kingdom of

The Saudi Arabian flag is distinctive in both its
simplicity of design and its featuring of an inscription
as its central motif. The inscription reads, "There is no
god but Allah and Mohammed is the prophet of
Allah." This is the *shahada,* or Muslim creed. Two copies
of the flag are stitched back to back, so that the inscription can be read on the obverse and reverse sides, and
the hilt of the sword always appears in the fly, at the
start of the inscription. The sword commemorates the
victories of Ibn Saud which were responsible for the
unification of the kingdom with its present boundaries,
in the first half of this century. The green of the field
represents both the Islamic religion and the Wahabi
sect, influential in the late 19th and early 20th
centuries.

# SENEGAL, Republic of

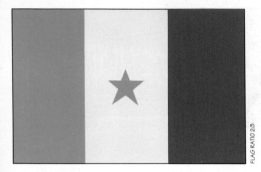

Senegal, in federation with neighboring Mali, became independent of France in 1960, and broke up the federation thereafter. Senegal retained the basic design of the federation flag – a tricolor, based on the that of the French, in the Pan-African colors green, yellow and red, signifying African unity and solidarity. The only modification was the removal of a black stick-figure which then featured in the center of the Mali flag and its replacement with a green five-pointed star, representing the opening of the country to the five continents. The flag was officially adopted in 1960.

# SEYCHELLES, Republic of

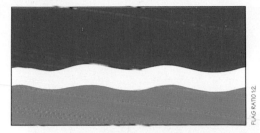

FLAG RATIO 1:2

The Seychelles has had two flags in the short period of its independence: the first lasted one year (1976–77) before a coup d'état replaced both government and flag. The People's United Party – later the People's Progressive Front – formed the new government and adapted their own flag as the new national one. The red band represents both revolution and progress towards a fair and equitable society, the green symbolizes agriculture, main source of wealth of the islands, and the wavy white band depicts the Indian Ocean around the archipelago, and the natural and mineral resources in it. Together, the three colors symbolize the unity and aspirations of the islanders.

# SIERRA LEONE, Republic of

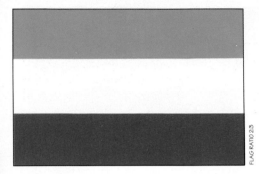

FLAG RATIO 2:3

Sierra Leone was the first African nation set up as a haven for freed slaves, in 1787, although subsequently it became a British colony. The national flag, a horizontal tricolor of green, white and blue symbolizes various aspects and attributes of the country. The green band represents the country's agriculture, and the characteristic vegetation of its wooded slopes; the white stands for peace and justice; and the blue symbolizes the waters of the Atlantic. The flag was adopted in 1961 when Sierra Leone became independent of Britain.

# SINGAPORE, Republic of

FLAG RATIO 2:3

The red and white used in the Singapore flag are colors which appear often in the flags of Southeast Asia. In this instance, the red stands for universal brotherhood and equality of man, and the white for everlasting purity and virtue. The crescent represents the young nation's ascent, guided by the five stars of democracy, peace, progress, justice and equality. It was adopted in 1959 when Singapore was still a British colony and was retained when it became independent in 1965, having joined and left the Malaysian Federation in the intervening years.

# SLOVAKIA, Republic of

FLAG RATIO 2:3

Slovakia's flag dates originally from 1848, the year of revolutions in Europe and of the Slavic desire for self-determination from the Austro-Hungarian Empire, and its tricolor of white, blue and red bears the traditional Slav colors. It had been used as the flag of an independent Slovakia only during the Second World War, when Czechoslovakia broke up. Slovakia became independent again when, almost three years after regaining its independence from Soviet control, the Czech and Slovak Federal Republic split in January 1993. In this version of the national flag, however, the arms are set near the hoist, to distinguish the flag from those of Russia and Slovenia. The arms, with their double cross set upon the central hill of three hills, are based on a part of the Hungarian arms, although the symbolism has altered.

# SLOVENIA, Republic of

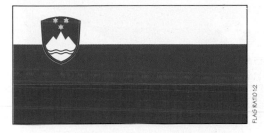

FLAG RATIO 1:2

The colors of the Slovenian flag are the Pan-Slav white, blue and red. The flag had its origins in the Russian tricolor at a time in the mid 19th century when the Slav states were trying to use the power of Russia as a counterweight against the Hapsburgs to win a measure of home rule from the Austro-Hungarian Empire. With the empire's decline at the end of the First World War in 1918, the southern Slav states were formed into the new state which was ultimately called Yugoslavia. However, the decline of European Communism in the late 1980s removed the threads which had bound the disparate elements of the federation together, and Slovenia and Croatia broke away from the Yugoslavian federation in 1991. Slovenia adopted the traditional tricolor, now with the shield of arms in the canton, as its new national flag.

# SOLOMON ISLANDS

FLAG RATIO 1:2

This flag was adopted in 1977 in anticipation of independence the following year, after almost a century of colonial rule, first by Germany and then by Britain. Its colors are symbolic, representing the sea (blue), the land (green) and sunshine (yellow). The five stars represent the five districts into which the islands were previously divided (there are now eight districts, but this is not yet reflected in the flag). The colors of the flag are also dominant in the national arms, which were adopted at the same time.

# SOMALIA, Somal Democratic Republic

FLAG RATIO 2:3

Somalia was formed by a union in 1960 of British Somalia and Italian Somaliland, the latter a United Nations Trust Territory from 1950. The present flag was adopted by the Italian, southern part of the country in 1954 and is based on the colors of the UN flag. On the establishment of the unified state in 1960, it was adopted as the national flag. The star is a symbol of liberty, and its five points represent the five areas in which the Somali peoples live: the two former regions, now united; Djibouti; northern Kenya; and southern Ethiopia.

# SOUTH AFRICA, Republic of

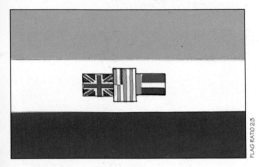

FLAG RATIO 2:3

The colors of the Dutch House of Orange were used as
the basis for the South African flag, in commemoration
of the first white settlers to reach the country from the
United Provinces in the mid 17th century: reputedly,
this flag was raised by Jan van Riebeeck, founder of
the Cape settlement, when he landed there in 1652. It
was also intended that the flag should be one which
could reconcile the opposing British and Boer factions
in the wake of the bitter divisions of the Boer Wars of
the late 19th century, so the charge of three smaller
flags in the white band are the flags of Britain
(representing the former British provinces of Cape and
Natal), the Orange Free State and the Transvaal (both
former Boer republics). The flag was first adopted in
1928, and was retained after South Africa left the
Commonwealth and became a republic in 1961.

# SPAIN

FLAG RATIO 2:3

The red and yellow associated with Spain are taken
from the arms of the provinces of Castile and Aragon,
and were first used in the flag in 1785. However, they
have been used in the current design only since 1939,
when the Fascist victors of the Civil War (1936–39) did
away with the republican government's flag of a red,
yellow and purple horizontal tricolor. The state flag
has the arms set towards the hoist in the yellow band.
These were modified 1981 and comprise, in a shield,
the arms of Castile, León, Aragon, Navarre and
Granada, with the badge of the royal House of Bourbon
(three *fleurs de lis*) in the center. The shield is topped by
a crown and bordered by the two Pillars of Hercules,
the boundaries of the ancient world; these have the sea
at their base and, wound around them, a scroll reading
Plus Ultra (More Beyond), a reference to overseas
exploration and the Spanish American Empire.

# SRI LANKA, Democratic Socialist Republic of

FLAG RATIO 5:9

The design of this flag has evolved gradually in an attempt to achieve national unity since the country, then known as Ceylon, gained its independence from Britain in 1948. Originally, the flag's central emblem was a gold lion and sword on a red field, derived from the flag of the Sinhalese kingdom of Kandy. As a consequence, it was not popular with minority groups in the country, and so was amended in 1951 to include a green and an orange band, to represent the Muslim and Tamil communities respectively. Finally, when the country adopted the local name of Sri Lanka in 1972, the flag was modified once more, with four leaves of the *pipul* tree, a Buddhist symbol, being added to the four corners of the dark red panel. This version of the flag was in official use from 1978.

# SUDAN, Republic of the

FLAG RATIO 1:2

The Pan-Arab colors were adopted for the current flag of Sudan in 1970, after a revolution brought down the existing government and led to the abandoning of the national flag – a blue, yellow and green horizontal tricolor – used since independence from Anglo-Egyptian control in 1956. The new colors were expressive of Arab nationalism and were the colors of the new ruling party, but they were also intended to be of significance in their own right: red for the independence struggle; white for peace; black for the nation; and green for prosperity and the Islamic religion.

# SURINAM, Republic of

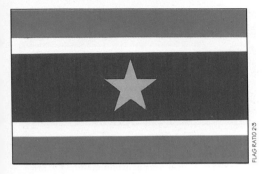

FLAG RATIO 2:3

Surinam, formerly Dutch Guiana, became independent in 1975, and its flag dates from that period. It superseded a previous flag, adopted in 1959, which comprised a white field with five stars of white, black, brown, yellow and red, representing the country's racial diversity. The colors of the three main political parties at the time of independence were used in the new flag, with the green, white and red now representing fertility, justice and freedom, and renewal respectively. The flag's central feature, a gold star, is a symbol of national sacrifice, unity and hope for the nation's golden future. This star echoes a yellow star which appears in the center of the national arms, dating originally from the 17th century but revised in 1959.

# SWAZILAND, Kingdom of

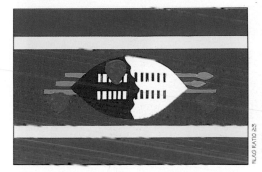

FLAG RATIO 2:3

The central emblem of the distinctive flag of Swaziland depicts the weapons of an Emasotsha warrior: a hide shield, two *assegai*, or spears, and a staff. Also featured are the blue plumes of a widowbird, traditionally regarded as Swazi royal ornaments. The background to the emblem is taken from the flag of the Swazi Pioneer Corps, who served with the British Army in the Second World War. Swaziland regained its independence from Britain in 1968, and the new flag had been adopted in the preceding year.

# SWEDEN, Kingdom of

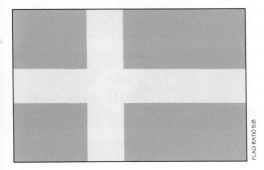

FLAG RATIO 5:8

1906 saw the official adoption of the present flag of Sweden, but it had first been used in a similar form almost four centuries before then: the oldest recorded pictures of a blue cloth with a yellow cross date from the 16th century. Its colors were probably taken from the national coat of arms, of three gold crowns on a blue field, which originated in the 14th century. Like Norway, Finland and Iceland, Sweden fell under Danish influence in the middle ages, and the design of its flag may be based on that of the Danes, with the off-center Scandinavian cross marking it immediately as one of the Norse nations. Like Iceland, Finland, Norway and Denmark, its naval ensign is of the distinctive swallowtail or swallowtail-with-tongue shape.

# SWITZERLAND,
## Swiss Confederation

FLAG RATIO 1:1

Although the flag of Switzerland was not officially
adopted until 1848, it had actually been in use as the
Swiss emblem since the 14th century. It was the banner
of Schwyz, one of the original three cantons who
founded the Confederation in 1291 for mutual self-
defence against the Hapsburgs. At the Battle of
Laupern in 1339 it was used to distinguish the soldiers
of the Confederation from their opponents. Although
the country was occupied by Napoleonic France from
1798–1815, its neutrality was ultimately guaranteed
under the 1815 Treaty of Paris.

# SYRIA, Syrian Arab Republic

FLAG RATIO 2:3

Syria has changed its flag a surprising five times in under 50 years as an independent state. The colors used in all its six flags so far have always been those of the Pan-Arab movement (black, white, red and green), used initially by many Arab regions as an anti-Ottoman nationalist device, and then after the collapse of the Ottoman Empire as an expression of Arab solidarity. Each flag change has reflected contemporary Syrian alliances, and the current one, which has been in use since 1980, was first used in 1958 when Syria and Egypt formed the United Arab Republic, a coupling from which Syria seceded in 1961. The two stars represented the two member states.

# TADZHIKISTAN, Republic of

Tadzhikistan was the last of the old republics of the USSR to adopt a new flag. To date, limited information is available about the significance of the design, which features a gold crown and an arc of seven stars centered in a white band, with bands of red and green above and below. The colors of red, white and green are the same as those chosen in 1953 for the flag of the Tadzhik Soviet Socialist Republic, this featured a red flag with a band of white and a smaller band of green. The new flag was adopted in November 1992.

# TANZANIA, United Republic of

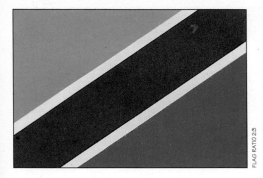

FLAG RATIO 2:3

Tanzania was formed in 1964 following the union of
the two newly independent states of Tanganyika (1961)
and Zanzibar (1963), and the flag of the new state took
elements from both the old ones. The flag of
Tanganyika on independence had been a green, black
and green horizontal triband, with yellow fimbriations
on the green band. Zanzibar's was a horizontal tricolor
of blue, black and green. The new flag kept the colors
in common, with the addition of the Zanzibarian blue,
all arranged in a diagonal rather than horizontal
pattern. The colors are said to represent the land
(green), mineral wealth (yellow), the people (black),
and the sea (blue).

# THAILAND, Kingdom of

FLAG RATIO 2:3

The Trairong (tricolor), the national flag of Thailand, has been in use since 1917. The country was the ancient Kingdom of Siam, and the flag until 1916 comprised a white elephant (the national emblem) on a red field. A simpler flag, retaining only the colors in the form of stripes, was designed in 1916, and in 1917 the blue stripe was added to the center. The blue stripe is taken to signify the monarchy, the white symbolizes the purity of Buddhism, the national religion, while the red stands for the life blood of the peoples. Siam's name was changed to Thailand in 1939, but the Trairong was retained.

# TOGO, Togolese Republic

FLAG RATIO 3:5

Like so many other West African states, the flag of
Togo uses the Pan-African colors, first adopted by
neighboring Ghana, as an expression of African unity.
In Togo's case, the colors are meant also to be
significant in their own right: green representing both
hope and agriculture, one of the mainstays of the
economy; yellow, for the country's mineral deposits;
and red symbolizing the independence struggle. The
star on the Togo flag is white rather than the black
normally used on African flags, and represents
national purity. The flag was adopted in 1960, on the
country's independence from France.

# TONGA, Kingdom of

FLAG RATIO 1:2

The Kingdom of Tonga was established in the mid 19th century, and its flag was designed shortly thereafter. It was officially adopted in 1875 on the understanding that it would never be changed. The red field with its white canton and red couped cross (one whose arms do not extend to the edges of its field) all represent the sacrifice and blood of Christ, and express the islanders' absolute commitment to Wesleyan Methodism. The islands became a British protectorate in 1900 but regained their independence in 1970, and retained their flag.

# TRINIDAD AND TOBAGO, Republic of

FLAG RATIO 3.5

The flag of Trinidad and Tobago dates officially from the time of the islands' independence from Britain (1962) and its colors are of symbolic significance. Red represents the vitality of the land and people and the energy and warmth of the sun; black symbolizes the people's dedication and unity of purpose, and the wealth of the land; while white stands for the sea which bounds the islands, the purity of national aspirations, and the equality of all. Together, then, the colors represent the elements of fire, earth and water encompassing the islands. The same colors are used in the shield of the national arms, which were also adopted at the time of independence.

# TUNISIA, Republic of

FLAG RATIO 2:3

Tunisia's flag was designed deliberately to look like that of Turkey. The Turks controlled the country from the 16th century, and the flag was adopted in 1835 with the intention of identifying Tunisia as an Ottoman possession. The crescent and star are traditional Ottoman as well as Islamic symbols. The flag survived throughout the French Protectorate (1881 1956) and was retained on independence in 1956. As in the other French North African possessions, the tricolor did not influence the flag officially adopted after independence.

# TURKEY, Republic of

FLAG RATIO 2:3

Turkey's white crescent moon and five-pointed star on a red field, is one of the most distinctive of flags. It evolved finally into its present shape in the last century. Red was the traditional color of the Ottoman Empire, of which Turkey was the heart, and although the star and crescent have come to be identified as Islamic symbols, their origins are obscure, and they may well pre-date both Islam and Christianity, in which they also have a significance. Despite its imperial association, the flag was retained in 1923 by Mustafa Kemel, renamed Ataturk, under whose leadership the country became a modern, secular republic.

# TURKMENISTAN, Republic of

FLAG RATIO 1:2

Turkmenistan's new flag was adopted in 1992, shortly after the break-up of the Union of Soviet Socialist Republics, of which the country had been a part. Its green field and crescent moon identify the country immediately as Islamic in religion. The elaborate band in the hoist is a detailed depiction of a red Turkistani carpet. The five patterns on the carpet stand for the five main tribes, representing the disparate elements of the republic. These five elements are repeated in the stars which appear by the crescent.

# TUVALU

FLAG RATIO 1:2

Together with the islands now known as Kiribati, Tuvalu (as the Gilbert and Ellice Islands) was a colony of Britain until 1975. The Ellice Islands broke away from the Gilberts in 1975 to become completely independent in its own right, as Tuvalu, in 1978. The flag was adopted on independence: a pale Blue Ensign shows the islands' continued close links with Britain, while the nine gold stars ranged across the fly represent the islands of the group. The name "Tuvalu" actually means "eight islands", as opposed to the nine, as one is uninhabited, but the nine are depicted nevertheless on the flag.

# UGANDA, Republic of

FLAG RATIO 2:3

The flag of Uganda was adopted on independence from Britain in 1962 and, despite four coups since then, has remained the same to the present day. It comprises six equal horizontal bands of black, yellow and red, and the colors are symbolic: black represents the people; yellow stands for the sun, which shines directly overhead in this equatorial country; and red represents the brotherhood of all peoples. The central white disc is charged with a crested crane.

# UKRAINE, Republic of

FLAG RATIO 1:2

The blue and yellow bicolor of the Ukraine has a background firmly rooted in the republic's history. The colors appeared on the coat of arms of one of the medieval Ukranian kingdoms, as well as being used on banners in the fight to expel invading Mongol forces in the 13th century. The colors resurfaced in modern times in 1848, when the Ukraine was one of the few countries involved in the Pan-Slav movement not to adopt the Russian colors. As well as having heraldic and historical interpretations, the flag's colors also have a popular explanation: the blue represents the sky, while the yellow symbolizes the golden wheat of the Steppes plains. Independence for the whole region came with the disintegration of the old empires at the end of the First World War, and the bicolor was officially adopted just before proclamation of the independent republic in 1918. The flag was readopted by the Ukranian parliament in 1991 at the break-up of the Union of Soviet Socialist Republics, of which the Ukraine had been a part.

# UNITED ARAB EMIRATES

FLAG RATIO 1:2

Red was traditionally the color used to represent the
Kharijite peoples of Southeast Arabia, together with
white, which was used on their flags by most of the
states in this part of the Persian Gulf, following a
maritime treaty with Britain in 1820. Consequently, red
and white were the colors of the flags in six of the
seven sheikdoms which came to form the United Arab
Emirates in 1971. All seven member states – Abu
Dhabi, Dubai, Sharjah, Rasal Khaimah, Fujeirah,
Ajman and Umm al Qaiwan – still retain their own
flags and arms, but the United Arab Emirates has
adopted the colors of the Pan-Arab movement – red,
green, white and black – expressive of Arab
nationalism and unity, and, of course, having the
common red and white colors shared by the individual
states.

# UNITED KINGDOM of Great Britain and Northern Ireland

FLAG RATIO 1:2

The Union Flag, or Union Jack as it is commonly if incorrectly known, is a combination of the flags of England, Scotland and Ireland. It first emerged in a recognizable form in 1603 after the accession of James VI of Scotland to the throne of England. A jack reflecting the unity of the two countries under the king was deemed necessary for shipping, and on April 12, 1606 the first Union Jack, combining the blue-on-white saltire of St. Andrew and red-on-white cross of St. George, was used. A white fimbriation separated the red from the blue. A saltire which was supposed to represent St. Patrick and Ireland was included on January 1, 1801 when Ireland was brought fully into the Union, although this flag was counterchanged to give precedence to that of Scotland.

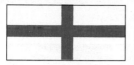

### England

The cross of St. George was first used by the Crusaders and was fully established as the emblem of England by the 16th century.

### Northern Ireland

The Red Hand of Ulster reflects local links with England in the cross of St. George, while the red hand is the traditional symbol of Ulster, legend identifying it as the bloody hand of Hugh O'Neil which he cut off to throw to the shore in the race from England to be the first to touch land, thereby winning the province. The six pointed star represents the six counties in Northern Ireland, and the crown symbolizes the union with Britain. This ceased to be the official flag in 1974, and is used only by the Loyalist faction in Northern Ireland.

### Scotland

The centuries-old cross of St. Andrew is based on the x-shaped cross on which the patron saint of Scotland was crucified. His bones were reputedly brought ashore at St. Andrews in Scotland, from the Holy Land.

### Wales

Wales had been ruled with England since its annexation in the 13th century and consequently its flag did not feature in the Union Jack. However, the Red Dragon of Cadwallader, Prince of Gwynedd, was recognized as Wales's official flag in 1959. The white and green field represents the colors of Prince Llewellyn of Wales.

### Isle of Man

The Manx flag is of medieval origin and shows a trinacria, or Three Legs emblem, on a red field. The legs run clockwise on both the obverse and reverse sides of the flag.

### Alderney (Channel Islands)

The cross of St. George has the addition of a badge of green in its center, encircling a crowned lion rampant which is holding a branch.

*Guernsey (Channel Islands)*

The cross of St. George contains a gold cross, added in 1985, from the banner of William the Conqueror who united Normandy, England and the Channel Islands.

*Jersey (Channel Islands)*

Jersey's flag resembles that attributed to St. Patrick and Ireland on the Union Jack, with the saltire here surmounted by a crowned shield bearing the arms of Jersey. The shield was added in 1981.

*Sark (Channel Islands)*

The island's unofficial flag has the cross of St. George with two gold lions from the Duchy of Normandy's coat of arms, on a red canton.

# UNITED STATES OF AMERICA

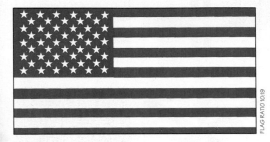

FLAG RATIO 10:19

The flag of the USA has evolved gradually from the original version in 1775 when it was a British colony. It is unclear how the design of stripes and stars came to be used, although it is probable that the basic design was a British ensign, with the Union Jack in the canton. Following the Declaration of Independence in 1776, the flag comprised 13 stripes and 13 stars, to represent the colonies then in revolt. It was originally intended that each new member of the union should be represented by a star and a stripe on the flag, but this soon proved impractical, and in 1818 it was decided that the original 13 stripes should remain, with a star only being added for each new state. The flag has been through 28 versions, the most recent being in 1960, after Hawaii joined the union. Like the French tricolor, the Stars and Stripes has been influential in the design of other flags: its colors were seen as representing revolution and freedom, and stripes and stars, rarely used in flags before this one, have since become among the commonest vexillological design features.

1795 Flag

District of Columbia

Alabama

Alaska

Arizona

Arkansas

CALIFORNIA REPUBLIC

California

Colorado

Connecticut

Delaware

Florida

Georgia

Hawaii

Idaho

Illinois

Indiana

Iowa

Kansas

Kentucky

Louisiana

Maine

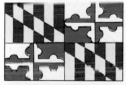

Maryland

Massachusetts

Michigan

223

Minnesota

Mississippi

Missouri

Montana

Nebraska

Nevada

New Hampshire

New Jersey

New Mexico

New York

North Carolina

North Dakota

Ohio

Oklahoma

Oregon

Pennsylvania

Rhode Island

South Carolina

South Dakota

Tennessee

Texas

Utah

Vermont

Virginia

Washington

West Virginia

Wisconsin

Wyoming

# URUGUAY, Oriental Republic of

FLAG RATIO 2:3

Uruguay's history throughout the 19th century was dominated by a struggle to retain its independence from both Brazil and Argentina, after gaining its freedom from Spanish colonial rule. The present flag was adopted in 1830, and its blue and white stripes are similar to those on the flags of other South and Central American countries. The nine stripes represent the nine original provinces of the country, and the sun is a symbol of independence, again like that on other South American flags. Uruguay's original emblem was the flag of José Artigas, the national hero who first tried in the early 19th century to free the country from Spanish rule, and this now forms the jack: a blue, white and blue triband with a red diagonal stripe running from top of hoist to foot of fly.

# UZBEKISTAN, Republic of

FLAG RATIO 1:2

The new flag of the republic, formerly a part of the
Union of Soviet Socialist Republics, was adopted in
1991. Its colors are symbolic: the blue stands for
Uzbekistan's waters and skies, the white for peace, and
the green for fertility and nature. The crescent and stars
are traditional Muslim symbols, and the 12 stars here
are symbolic of the months of the Islamic calendar. The
blue color also recalls the color of Timur, a former
khan, under whose rule in the 14th century the whole
region enjoyed a golden age of expansion and
prosperity.

# VANUATU, Republic of

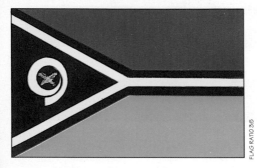

FLAG RATIO 3:5

This Pacific archipelago was ruled jointly by France and Britain until 1980 as the New Hebrides. On independence, the country's name was changed and a new flag was adopted, whose colors were also those of the Vanuaaku Pati, the leading political party of the time. The yellow "Y" on its side, which runs the full length of the flag, is a reference to the fact that the islands lie in a "Y" shape. The emblems in the black triangle at the hoist are a boar's tusk, a local emblem, and, inside it, two crossed fern or *namele* leaves, representing the traditional way of life of the people of the islands.

# VATICAN, State of the Vatican City

FLAG RATIO 1:1

The colors of the Vatican flag are taken from the emblem which appears in the fly of the yellow and white bicolor. They were adopted as the papal colors by Pius VII in 1808, and the flag was used from 1825–70, until the unification of Italy when all separate provinces in the country, including the Papal States, were joined. With the Lateran Treaty of 1929, the Papal States received an acknowledgement from Italy of its right to a separate existence again, although confined to the Vatican City. The emblem itself shows the three-tiered papal crown, signifying the three types of temporal powers – legislative, executive and judicial – vested in the pope, while the crossed keys below symbolize his spiritual authority from the bestowing of the keys of the kingdom of Heaven by Christ on St. Peter, the first pope.

# VENEZUELA, Republic of

FLAG RATIO 2:3

Venezuela, Colombia and Ecuador have similar flags, all three having adopted the 1806 flag of Francisco de Miranda, whose attempts to liberate South America from Spanish colonial rule were taken up, with the flag, by Simón Bolívar in 1811, this time successfully. The three countries were joined in federation, as Gran Colombia, from 1819 to 1830. In 1836 the proportions of the bands on the Venezuelan flag were made equal to distinguish it from that of Colombia and Ecuador. The colors originally denoted the golden land of South America (yellow) separated from imperial Spain (red) by the sea (blue). The seven stars represent the original provinces of the country. The addition of the arms to the canton gives the state flag: a shield containing a scene depicting the land and its independence, is surmounted by two cornucopiae spilling out natural bounty. Dates on a scroll below commemorate independence and the adoption of a federal constitution.

# VIETNAM, Socialist Republic of

FLAG RATIO 2:5

Vietnam, as part of French Indochina, was occupied by the Japanese during the Second World War, and the ultimately victorious national resistance movement, led by Ho Chi Minh, adopted the flag they had used during the war, as the national flag in 1945. This was basically the same as the flag in use today, itself obviously influenced by the old Soviet flag, with the star of Communism in the center. The country was partitioned into north and south after the French left in 1954, and the government in the north began a long war to overcome the southern government and their American allies, and reunite the country, their aims finally being achieved in 1976.

# VIRGIN ISLANDS OF THE UNITED STATES

As their name suggests, the Virgin Islands of the US are an American dependency. They were bought from Denmark in 1917, and this territorial flag has been used since 1921. In the center of the white field is an emblem based on the US coat of arms, consisting of an American eagle with wings outstretched and on its breast a shield containing 13 vertical stripes in red and white beneath a blue chief (the top part of the shield). In its claws are an olive branch to symbolize peace, and three arrows, representing defence. The emblem appears between the initial letters of the islands' name, "V" and "I" in blue.

# WESTERN SAMOA,
## Independent State of

FLAG RATIO 1:2

Western Samoa passed from German control after the First World War to be administered by New Zealand as a League of Nations then United Nations Trust Territory. In the first version of the islands' flag, adopted in 1948, the cross in the canton had four stars, like that on the New Zealand flag, but this was changed to five in 1949, and this design was retained when the islands regained full independence in 1962. Red and white were colors used in Samoan flags in the precolonial period. Now, red stands for the blood shed in the struggle for independence, and blue for the unity of the nation. In common with other countries of the southern hemisphere, Western Samoa uses the distinctive constellation of the Southern Cross as the central motif of its flag and here, it indicates the islands' location in the Pacific.

# YEMEN, *Republic of*

FLAG RATIO 2:3

The former states of the Yemen Arab Republic (North Yemen) and the People's Democratic Republic of Yemen (South Yemen) united on May 22, 1990, and the country's new flag is an amalgamation of the flags of the two previously independent nations. The red, white and black tricolor shows the country's subscription to the Pan-Arab ideals of Arab nationalism and unity. The green star from the flag of the Yemen Arab Republic, and the blue triangle and red star from the flag of the People's Democratic Republic of Yemen, have both now been dropped. The flag's pattern is suggestive of a compromise between the officially secular former Yemen People's Democratic Republic and the more officially Islamic-orientated Yemen Arab Republic to the north.

# YUGOSLAVIA,
## Federal Republic of

FLAG RATIO 1:2

Its blue, white and red tricolor identifies Yugoslavia as
a Slavic state which was once a part of the Hapsburg
Empire. The Pan-Slav movement began in the first half
of the 19th century, and by 1848, the year of revolutions
in Europe, many of the old Slavic kingdoms and
provinces had adopted the white, blue and red of Russia,
in the hope of using the large power as a
counterbalance to the influence of Austria-Hungary.
The First World War brought to an end the sprawling
Hapsburg Empire, and the southern Slav states united
as Yugoslavia, adopting the tricolor as the national
flag. The new state was broken up by the Nazis, but
reunited under the victorious partisan leader, Tito, in
1945; for over 40 years following Tito's victory, the flag
carried a yellow-fimbriated red Communist star. But
the decline of European Communism in the late 1980s
and early '90s saw the fragmentation of the country
with Croatia, Slovenia and Bosnia-Herzegovina
breaking away, leaving only Serbia and Montenegro.
The star was dropped from the flag in 1992.

# ZAÏRE, Republic of

FLAG RATIO 2:3

Zaïre has had three flags since 1960 when, as the
Congo Free State, it became independent of Belgium.
The country suffered secession and civil war throughout the first part of the 1960s, but was reunited under
the Mouvement Populaire de la Révolution, acquiring
a new name and a new flag in 1971. The flag is based
on that of the ruling party, which also shows a hand
grasping a torch, and represents the revolutionary
spirit of the people. However, the main colors of the
national flag – green, yellow and red – are those of the
Pan-African movement, expressive of African unity
and solidarity.

# ZAMBIA, Republic of

FLAG RATIO 2:3

This national flag is unusual in that its distinguishing devices are set in the fly rather than in the hoist. Its colors are predominantly those of what was the major political party (United Nationalist Independence Party, or UNIP) in 1964 when Zambia, then Northern Rhodesia, won its independence. The interpretation now put on the colors is that the green field stands for agriculture, and the red, black and orange bars signify respectively the struggle for freedom, the people, and copper, the main national mineral resource. The eagle first appeared on the old colonial coat of arms but has now been adapted for the modern arms and for the flag, and symbolizes the national spirit, hopes for the future, and freedom.

# ZIMBABWE

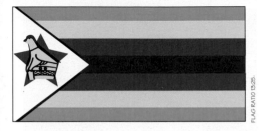

FLAG RATIO 13:25.

The seven stripes of the distinctive Zimbabwean flag echo the seven concentric rectangles of the same colors used by the Zimbabwe African National Union, which came to the fore from the alliance of the Patriotic Front to lead the country after the establishment of the new state in 1980 after the demise of Rhodesia. The colors in the flag are symbolic: green for agriculture; yellow for mineral wealth; red for the freedom struggle; and, at the center, black for the people. Red, yellow and green, often with black motifs, are also, of course, the colors of the Pan-African movement of African unity. The black-fimbriated white triangle on the hoist symbolizes peace and the red star the government's socialist principles. The bird is traditional, first found carved on soapstone in the ancient ruined city of Zimbabwe; it has been the national emblem for many years and represents a link with the nation's heritage.